ALSO BY BETH GUTCHEON
The Perfect Patchwork Primer

THE
QUILT DESIGN
WORKBOOK

THE QUILT DESIGN WORKBOOK

Beth and Jeffrey Gutcheon

The Alchemy Press
New York

PHOTOGRAPHY CREDITS:

COLOR PLATES by H. E. Mattison, Robert L. Weinreb, Ben Schonzeit, Eeva-Inkeri, Bevan Davies

BLACK-AND-WHITE PHOTOGRAPHS by Eeva-Inkeri, Ben Schonzeit, James Wardrop, Robert L. Weinreb, Jeffrey Gutcheon, Virginia Burroughs

Library of Congress Cataloging in Publication Data

Gutcheon, Beth Richardson.
  The quilt design workbook.
  Bibliography: p.
  Includes index.
  1. Quilting. I. Gutcheon, Jeffrey, joint author.
II. Title.
TT835.G88   746.9′7   76–13433
ISBN 0–89256–004–5

Published simultaneously in Canada by McClelland and Stewart, Ltd.
Manufactured in the United States of America
by Halliday Lithograph Corporation,
West Hanover, Massachusetts
Designed by Jeffrey Gutcheon and Evelyn O'Connor
Third Printing November 1979

For Michele Godbout
With our love

ACKNOWLEDGMENTS

Our thanks to Patsy and Myron Orlofsky and to Gail and Jonathan Holstein for scholarship, friendship, and especially for all they have contributed to our knowledge of American quiltmaking. Thanks to Molly Upton and Sue Hoffman, Rose Dwight, and Virginia Avery for allowing their work to appear here, and for all the pleasure their work has given us. Thanks to Wendy Weil, to Evelyn O'Connor and to Eleanor Rawson, for advice, assistance and support. Thank you Rudi. Thank you Buford. Thanks to Max and Laurie Munn, Debbie and Joel Freedman, Ben and Marcia Schonzeit, Bill and Carol Webb, and Penny and Ted Landreth, and so many friends and relations who were there when we needed them during the Year of the Hare. And to David Stray Gutcheon, for all the growing up we've done together.

Contents

List of Illustrations

How We Got into Quiltmaking

Before I get myself fairly launched, perhaps I should explain that the person writing the words is Beth Gutcheon. Jeffrey is making the pictures. We both make the quilts, although not every quilt is made by both of us. I usually try hard not to speak for Jeffrey since he doesn't like it, but in this case I'm going to because we can't both write at the same time and we can't exchange tasks because while Jeffrey can express himself in plain English, I cannot make a convincing picture of a square. As a compromise, Jeffrey looks over my shoulder now and then to encourage or complain.

Quiltmaking has been a great joy to us, and it has been many things to us at different times. I'm in favor of joy and would like to explain what I mean about quiltmaking in case I can manage to spread some of it to you. But I find that to talk about quiltmaking in our lives, I must talk about choices, so I think I'd better start by explaining how I feel about those.

I have a brother-in-law who thinks I'm a hippie. He thinks this in spite of the fact that I've been married to the same man for eight years and have a son, a life-insurance policy, and a mortgage, and prefer white wine to all other drugs. The reason he thinks I'm a hippie is partly that I work at home instead of putting on shoes and socks and going to an office like a real grown-up, and partly that we live in a loft in downtown New York, which he considers tantamount to living in a tree. Never mind that *New York* magazine calls our neighborhood "Manhattan's exciting artists' district." *He* knows that's media hooey. What he sees is that we live in a big queer space with no completely enclosed rooms except the bathroom, with plaster dust sifting gently from the walls each time the BMT roars by beneath our street, and with a table saw in the dining room.

Once, because I was asked to, I wrote an article about our marriage—about how we try to share the financial responsibilities, how we decide whose turn it is to worry about the fur balls under the sofa, and things like that. After it came out, an old friend of mine greeted me warmly at a Christmas party with the news that she had read my article and disliked it very much. She felt, it seems, that by making a series of choices that were quite unlike the sort she had made, I was on some level criticizing her way of being. I wanted to tell her (though I don't believe I did) that her way of being seems wonderful to me but that it just wasn't a choice that was available to me. She has a much firmer faith in individual autonomy than I do. I don't believe life is a gay, mad smorgasbord in which you can serve yourself with absolutely anything. I think instead that people attract what they need in this life, and even if it is not immediately apparent *why* they needed what they got, that doesn't mean that they could, by simple force of character, have turned out entirely different. I certainly haven't made any choice with the thought that it was a superior way of being, but simply from the hope that it would suit me and the people in my life. And I sincerely hope that my brother-in-law has not bought a house in West Hartford and joined a golf club with an eye toward embarrassing *me*.

Jeffrey and I live in a loft because at some point, years before we moved down here, we made the decision to try to remain self-employed as long as possible. We liked working at home, we liked being together, and we found that staying very close at all times helped to keep out the dark. Jeffrey was doing one architecture project every year or so, but mostly he was devoting his time to becoming a rock-and-roll star. I was reading and writing and teaching myself how to sew. We both needed a lot of space because we were both living and working on several things in the same place. We had lived in two rooms on First Avenue above a vegetable market, but when David was born, we bought a loft in a deserted neighborhood downtown. It was big and cheap because at the time it was illegal to live there. The area was zoned for light industry, which means sweat shops. Our place had nothing in it whatsoever except dirt, a cold-water riser, and marks from ancient flatirons burned into the floor. In our neighborhood moving into a place like that and fixing it for human habitation is called pioneering your space.

Our decisions to be self-employed came about this way: Jeffrey had a degree in architecture from MIT and had put in his time working in offices. But he found that while he loved design—doing it, teaching it, and talking about it—the realities of working as an architect had very little to do with designing and a great deal to do with compromise, frustration, and almost unendurable delay between the completion of a design and its becoming a building. Besides, since a recession hits building trades first and relieves them last, practically everybody he went to architecture school with is unemployed now except for the one who made a million dollars making picture frames. So he decided to become a piano player instead, and that worked out very well. You've probably heard him on the radio and never even knew it.

As for me, as long as I remember, all I ever wanted in life

was to do things to books. Read them, write them, edit them—I didn't care. So when I finished college, I went to work for a small, distinguished publishing house. Although I am quite a good editor and an excruciatingly bad typist, I was made a secretary to two editors. One of them was extremely handsome, recently divorced, well connected, and chronically drunk. My job was that on Wednesday he would have me write a letter to some minor celebrity, the wife of a senator, an ex-athlete, or someone like that, saying he was coming to New York for the weekend and they should get together and discuss the possibility of the addressee writing a big gossipy memoir. Then on Monday he would dictate another letter saying, "Dear Gloria, I am so sorry I put the lampshade on my head just as the vice-president arrived, and I do hope the bishop wasn't offended when I took off my clothes. I had no idea he was a bishop. I hope you like the flowers. We must get together again sometime."

I was not a success as an editor's secretary.

When we moved to New York, I decided to try to write, but I had read too much Hemingway, and I thought that the way to write was to turn on your electric typewriter and drink *vin ordinaire* till you fell off your stool. So everything was very depressing, and I decided to have a baby.

The reason I'm telling you all this is that the truth is I did not come to quiltmaking because I had the slightest idea what it or any craft was about (in the beginning), and not, heaven knows, because I had any reason to think I was an artist. But I had arrived at a point where I felt I had a supporting role in the life of my husband and my son, and no life of my own at all. I needed something I could do in the irregular periods of slack time when the baby didn't need me (but I couldn't leave the house), something that would be real work, something that would challenge but not defeat me, something that would matter.

I think the urge to make things is very primitive—in fact, prehuman. There are little primates called lemurs that have scent glands, and as they go along from tree to tree, they leave little puddles of aroma saying to the next lemur to happen along, "I exist! I've passed this way!" Sometimes I see myself that way, going through life trailing quilts and pillows and things. They're nonverbal, they don't have to be explained, they just exist, and the fact that they exist proves that I exist. Perhaps someday people will see them and think, as I do when I see antique quilts now, "Some human being whose name I'll never know imagined this just this way, in these colors and no others, and then made it with her own warm living hands." Don't misunderstand me; I don't make quilts as a hedge against death. What I like is the general sense of continuity, the fact of communication between humans who know nothing about each other and who weren't even on earth at the same time. I don't make anything of it. I just like it.

Quiltmaking meant more to me than any other craft for many reasons. First, I could do it at home without special equipment. Second, the products of the craft are genuinely useful. Most important, there is no necessary connection between how good a patchwork design is and how hard it is to make. And that means that even the rankest beginner can do work that is not just not ridiculous but is *really* good. I liked it at once because it was not monotonous. You don't just repeat the same basic activity from beginning to end; you design the patchwork, you choose fabric, you cut, you sew, you press, you design a quilting pattern, then you quilt. You can do it by yourself, with your friends, or with your husband or your wife or your children. Sometimes you need one thing, sometimes the other.

When I first began, I had to reinvent the craft for myself because I couldn't find anyone in New York who knew any more about quilts than I did and because the old books on the subject were largely out of print (though many have since been reissued) and none of the new ones had been written yet. I think that was mostly an advantage, because out of sheer ignorance I discovered new ways to do certain things. When you learn something at your mother's knee and she learned it at her mother's knee, it's much harder to say to yourself, "There must be a better way to do this"—even if there is. I learned a great deal at my mother's knee, but fortunately none of it had anything to do with sewing. Jeffrey helped a lot in the beginning, even before he got involved as quiltmaker, because architects know a lot about drafting tools and how to trisect inches and plot curves, while I am a dead loss at geometry and all that. But most of it I worked out for myself, because to do piecework, you don't really have to know anything, you just have to be able to see.

Eventually I came to feel something more, though, about quiltmaking than that it was a good way for me to pass the time. I came to feel that American quilts are not just a series of artifacts but an important part of the history of American women. That their beauty, their ingenuity, and also the vast amount of repetition, the great number of cautious variations on familiar themes, in some important way constitutes a record of what life has been like for American women. Not the least important is the fact that while the quilts contain a great deal of testimony, almost all of it is mute. American women have long had hearts and minds, but only a very few have had voices.

I thought, for example, that there was something in the quilts worth learning about pain. About effort, about boredom, disappointment, frustration, loneliness. I felt that women who made patchwork knew what the blues makers knew: that pain is energy, that it can be used to make a speaking thing that will be remembered when the pain is forgotten. I felt also that in the history of quilts and how they were made at births and deaths and weddings, in the spring when the roads thawed and in the winters when country families were closed in for months together, there was much to learn about what mothers and daughters, sisters and cousins, aunts and nieces, and friends and neighbors have been to each other. I liked to think of the long hours of sitting together, working and talking and teaching each other. I don't want to be there, but I think it's good to think about it.

Jeffrey got interested in quilts because he realized that designing a quilt was not unlike other kinds of design he had been trained for, and making a quilt was not unlike building a chair. It's all a matter of space and color, the right tools and the right way to use them. He had long since given up pure architectural design in favor of projects he could design and then build with his own hammer—mostly interior renovations. For both of us the actual making was as important as having the idea. He especially liked quilts because, he says, most of us live our lives in spaces completely dominated by right angles. Streets, buildings, floors, walls, ceilings. Zulus don't; their huts are round. Plains Indians didn't. There isn't a right angle anywhere in a tipi. But our expectations about the right-angledness of the world are extremely intense. Someone once told me of an experiment she saw in a graduate psychology course in which the professor had built a small model house that had the expected angles and perspectives on three sides, but on the fourth all the angles were slightly off, the perspective slightly too long here, too short there. He put the model on a turntable and spun it slowly around, and everyone watching it became sick to his stomach. Jeffrey likes patchwork design because it gives him great pleasure to introduce so many different kinds of geometries besides right angles into the environment without making people sick.

The first year or two I was making quilts I had no idea why I was doing it, and it was perhaps the first non-goal-oriented activity I had ever undertaken in my life. I didn't care; I just loved it. Certainly I didn't imagine I would ever sell the quilts. The passion for antique quilts was just beginning at the time, and it was widely believed in the marketplace that the only good quiltmaker was a dead quiltmaker. Oh, I did have some commissions, and I made wedding presents for some friends and for my brothers and sisters—I have a lot of brothers and sisters—but I would have made the quilts anyway. Lately I heard someone say that a tree in the forest doesn't keep looking around at the other trees, wondering if it's growing faster or slower than they, or if it's all right to be putting down roots so deep instead of using its energy for making acorns—it just grows. That's its job—to grow. Only people drive themselves crazy asking, "What's this for? Am I doing all right? Am I doing better than someone else? Is it all right to be doing this?" Learning my craft and then practicing it, for no other reason than for itself, is one of the first steps I took in my life toward learning that growing is what life is for.

Inevitably, I suppose, my involvement with quiltmaking itself grew until it changed. The Holsteins' brilliant show of American piecework opened at the Whitney, our own work began to attract attention, and my friend Marcia, who has a gift for making connections for people, suggested that I should offer courses in quiltmaking. I had never thought of this because I am not a natural lesson taker myself; I am too afraid that I will turn out to be the dumbest person in the class and embarrass myself. Fortunately, New York turned out to be full of natural lesson takers, people who take course after course for the sheer fun of it. I say fortunately because quiltmaking has almost always been a shared, and a teaching, activity, and teaching quiltmaking became a central and enriching part of the craft for us.

When I was in college, there was a phrase we all knew: "Those who can, do, and those who can't, teach." I don't believe we thought about whether it was true or not; we just invoked it whenever necessary. I particularly remember the time I had worked very hard on a paper about the moral dilemmas of homicidal maniacs in Dostoevski and was awarded the only D of my career by a graduate student who not only had failed to grasp my point but also smeared jelly on the first page of the paper. I remember asserting that an instructorship in a small rural college was probably just the post in life she was suited for, but there's something I remember better about the whole event. I was actually very shaken and depressed about getting a D, and soon after, I ran into my friend Debby Hill, who asked me at once what was wrong with me. I explained the situation and said (more than half expecting to be contradicted) that deep in my heart I was afraid I really was a moron. And she replied with a rush of warmth, "Oh, I don't think that matters." It was a *wonderful* moment.

Anyway, as near as I can tell (living in the "exciting artists' district" I told you about), about half the artists with major reputations in America do, in fact, teach, even though their work commands five-figure prices. I think a majority of the important novelists of our generation do teach or have taught; I can name Mary McCarthy, John Barth, John Gardner, and Kurt Vonnegut without even stopping to think about it, but there are many more. And it's not just because they can't make a living making art; many of them can. Artists teach because art is a shared experience. You can make a painting or write a book all alone in your room, or go up on stage and play music, and somewhere out of time and space the experience of it is passed from the artist to the consumer of the art. But another way to share what you know and feel about your art is to teach, or to study with a teacher.

We've learned a lot about designing and making quilts in the course of years of teaching and lecturing, in the way that teachers have always learned from students. Partly it's because so many of the students are brilliant or imaginative in some way quite new to us, or else because they ask questions that we can't answer, forcing us to learn or invent some new way to solve a problem. But we've also learned something about the American tradition of quiltmaking by being a part of it, living.

For instance, in the beginning I believed that everyone's method of working on a quilt design would be just like mine, that if only I gave them all the separate parts of the quiltmaker's vocabulary and explained everything loudly and clearly, everyone would like to start from scratch and try to make some utterly new and unexpected design. And indeed, I found that many did, and that some went even further and eliminated the traditional vocabulary altogether, making things that are relatively flat and made of fabric, but not quilts or patchwork in any other sense. If forced to explain why I'm not so interested in that kind of work, I suppose I would fall back upon Robert Frost's remark about writing poetry without rhyme or meter: It's like playing tennis without a net. But of course that doesn't really prove anything except that I'm interested in a certain kind of discipline, or simply that I'm interested in what I'm interested in and not in everything else.

The other thing I learned is that some people do not want

to be given the separate pieces; they work better by making variations within a given framework. And upon looking into the matter I discovered that in fact many of the greatest quilts ever made are no more than this—a traditional, or borrowed, graphic outline, shaded or colored in a brilliant or subtle or original way. It was that discovery, coupled with the desire to share some new construction techniques we've hit upon in the years since my first book was written, that provided the impetus for us to make this book.

THE PATCHWORK TRADITION

The patchwork quilt is one of America's few truly indigenous art forms. Like jazz and the blues it has its roots in older cultures; Colonial women brought with them the crafts of piecing, patching, and quilting, but only here were these skills combined and transformed into a design tradition that has become world famous.

In the early years of the Colonies every scrap of fabric had to be saved because the Colonists were seriously undersupplied, exorbitant tariffs prevented their buying textiles from anywhere but England, and they were even required to pay a tax on any spinning or weaving they did for themselves. A Colonial woman always wore a sewing pocket tied around her waist in which she carried tools for cutting, mending, patching, and even for unraveling seams; instead of ripping the thread she would carefully wind it back onto an empty spool and use it again.

At first, American patchwork design was probably a matter of laying on a patch wherever the blanket developed a hole until the whole surface was covered with motley. But as soon as she could afford to, the Colonial woman began to cut her patches into regular geometric shapes that she could sew together to build into a mosaic pattern. Eventually it occurred to someone that instead of building the patchwork in one undifferentiated sheet, she could make a series of smaller lap-size units that would be joined into rows and then into a sheet at the end of the project. Using these repeating-design blocks made her work considerably more portable; it also permanently changed the look of piecework design.

During the eighteenth century, magnificent printed cottons were being imported by the East India Company of Calicutt (the origin of our word *calico*). British wool and flax merchants insisted upon crushing tariffs on these goods in both England and America, and this gave a special impetus to another magnificent tradition in American quilt design—the appliqué quilt. By carefully cutting out printed birds, flowers, butterflies, and bows and reapplying them to a large sheet of homespun in a formal pattern, a woman could make a yard of expensive chintz ornament into an entire quilt top.

A quilt is a textile sandwich; it has a top and bottom layer made of fabric, and a fluffy middle layer called filler or *batting*. The top may be plain or decorated with embroidery. It may be made from many small pieces sewn to one another to form a large sheet (*piecework*). Or it may be decorated with small pieces sewn onto a larger background piece (*appliqué*). Both piecework and appliqué are referred to as *patchwork*. When the top, batting, and backing of the quilt are assembled, they are then held together by lines of stitches called *quilting,* that go through all three layers and prevent them from shifting or bunching up.

HOW PATCHWORK DESIGNS WERE MADE

We know very little about how designs were made for the first two hundred years of our history. People didn't write about how to make quilts any more than you and I write down how to make toast. For one thing, reading and writing were not done with such thoughtless ease in those days, and for another, everyone already knew how quilts were made. Men and women had all learned the craft, or seen it practiced, from the time they were tiny children.

Nevertheless, we can intuit some things about early quilt design. We know from oral tradition that early block patterns were made by folding a square of paper. If you folded it in half and in half again, dividing the original block into four equal quadrants, you had a four-patch block, and if you folded it three times across and three down, dividing it into nine equal parts like a tic-tac-toe board, you had a nine-patch. These are the most common basic design types, though there are plenty of five-patch and seven-patch blocks as well, and there are also two- and one-patch patterns that we will deal with in a separate section.

Once you had made a basic four-patch, let us say, you could alter the design by folding again to add diagonal lines or rectangles or other geometric shapes, or you could cut the patches to create curves. When you were satisfied with your block, you cut out the paper shapes that comprised the design and made *templates* (cutting patterns) from them to guide you in tracing out the patchwork pieces with precision so they would all be the perfect size and shape. If then your neighbor (if you had a neighbor) admired the quilt, you would either give her your cutting patterns or let her use them to cut out the pieces to make one block so that she could later have a guide for reproducing your design. And when she came to make her own quilt, it would come out exactly the same as yours—the same design, the same scale, and often even the same colors. There were famous quilt patterns that were always done in white and red, for example, and if they were executed in some other combination, it was considered so innovative that the pattern was given a new name.

12

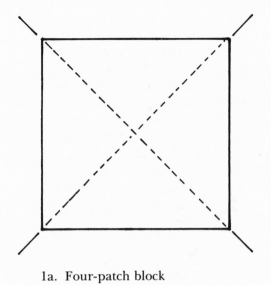

1a. Four-patch block

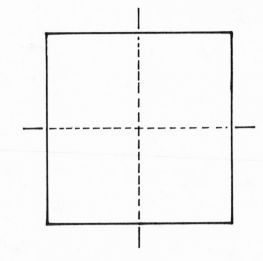

1b. Four-patch block

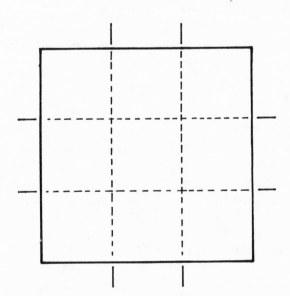

1c. Nine-patch block

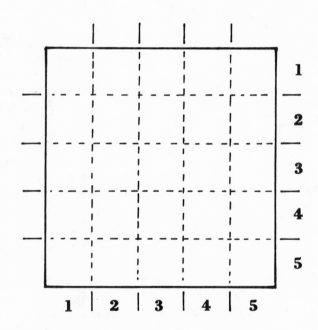

1d. "Five-patch" block

13

It is important to remember, I think, that of the hundreds of thousands of American women who have made patchwork throughout their lives, relatively few did so because it was thought to be "artistic." Most made quilts because if they didn't, their families would have frozen to death. Half of the Massachusetts Bay Colonists died of cold and hunger the first winter, and later, on the Great Plains, the pioneers found the winters commonly dipped to 40° below. Machine-made blankets weren't available until the 1870s. Colonial and pioneer women made handwoven coverlets, blankets, and bed rugs, but quilts were by far the most common protection against weather that could kill.

HOW QUILTING DESIGNS WERE MADE

For hundreds of years quilts have been stuffed with wool or, most often, cotton, though in hard times it was not uncommon to use leaves, paper, or corn husks. This filling had to be sewn in place to keep it from bunching up or lumping inside the quilt. The stitching that does this is called quilting. Quilting is definitely functional, though it also turned out to be decorative because it creates a bas-relief pattern on the fluffy surface of the quilt.

Quilting designs on masterpiece quilts tended to be very elaborate, with vines and scrolls and stuffed grape clusters all about; the point was to demonstrate the maker's patience and her skill as a needlewoman. It appears that the patterns themselves were often marked onto the quilt top by a professional, perhaps the local art teacher, much as people now buy expensive prepainted canvas for needlepoint. *Utility quilts* (those made for everyday use) were quilted in simpler patterns. Sometimes the quilter would coat a long string with chalk, then hold the string taut across the quilt (with the help of a friend on the other side). When she plucked the string, it left a long, straight chalk line across the patchwork. In this way she could quickly mark off the work in parallel lines or simple grids. At other times utility quilting simply followed the outline of the patchwork pattern; occasionally a template was used to mark a repetitive motif across the top of the quilt. Execution was more honored than originality, and most important of all was the consideration that if there were not a line of stitching every few inches, the quilt filler would roll itself into balls as soon as the quilt was washed.

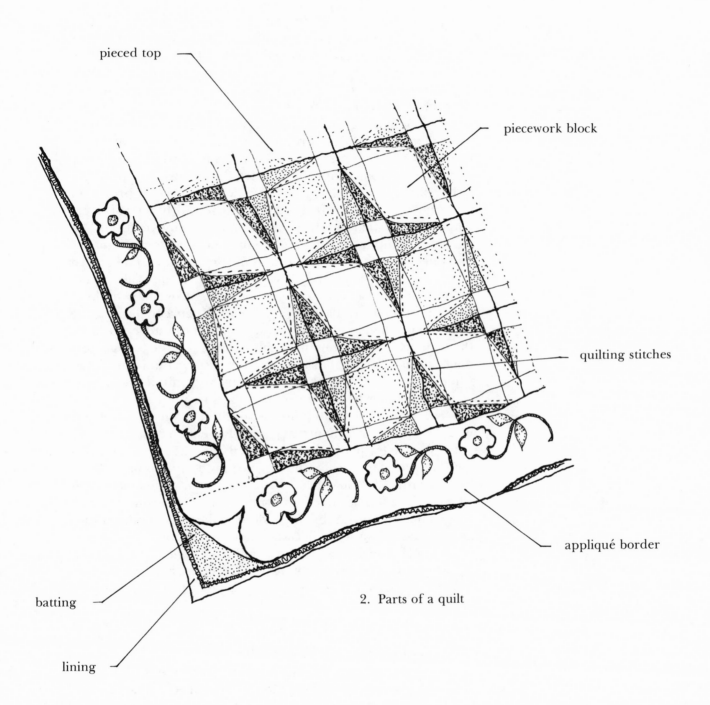

pieced top

piecework block

quilting stitches

appliqué border

batting

lining

2. Parts of a quilt

15

HOW PATCHWORK AND QUILTING
PATTERNS WERE PASSED ALONG

Quilting was, whenever possible, a social activity. Patchwork was more or less constantly made in the evenings or through the long winters when other work was at a minimum and the principal occupation was staying alive until spring. You did patchwork in your lap by the stove, by yourself or with your children. But when you had finished a top or two, if you could, you summoned a group of friends and neighbors to a quilting party. There were several reasons for this. The most important is that for many women, isolated from one another by weather and distance, sometimes for months, the opportunity to spend a day with other female grown-ups was a source of profound joy. Another reason was that quilts stuffed with natural fibers had to be stretched tightly on large frames during quilting. The frames took up a great deal of room, and since many families had only one or two heated rooms in winter, they could afford even less than you and I can to have a quilting frame monopolizing one of them for months. A woman quilting alone, picking up and leaving off her work between nursing the baby, doing the laundry in a pot boiling on the stove, running the mangle, and cooking the meals, might take weeks to get one quilt finished. But eight skilled quilters working uninterrupted while someone else cooked the meals and minded the baby could sometimes finish two simple quilts in a day.

Inevitably, since quilting was so often a communal affair, most everyone got a chance to pass judgment on everyone else's patchwork. New patterns were copied and passed on, and certain people, say Aunt Maudie, acquired the reputation of being artistic. People collected trunkfuls of sample blocks, and when Aunt Maudie invented a new one, it was something to write home about. But by the middle of the nineteenth century articles began to appear in *Godey's Lady's Book* complaining that young ladies no longer knew a quilting frame from a set of clothespoles, and as early as that, commercial patchwork patterns and even kits were advertised to take the place of Aunt Maudie.

CONTEMPORARY QUILT DESIGN

Modern quilt design has changed in a number of ways. First, the people who make quilts have changed. We are on the whole more literate, less housebound, and more likely to have at least some familiarity with the fine arts. These things affect

16

quilt design in that the modern quiltmaker is usually more interested in effective design than she is in proving that she can turn margins 1/16″ wide or take twelve quilting stitches to the inch, or spend forty years on a single piece of needlework. Craftsmanship remains important, of course, but it *is* craftsmanship, not something else. We choose designs for their aesthetic impact rather than for how fancy the sewing is going to be.

Second, technology has changed tremendously. The sewing machine has made it possible to sew in a few hours what formerly took days, and it does it stronger and better than most of us could manage by hand. The use of the sewing machine is a perfectly faithful development of a craft that was never leisure-time fancy work in the first place. From the moment home sewing machines became available in the early 1850s they were widely used for making patchwork. The sewing machine affects piecework design in that on a machine it is much easier and more accurate to assemble patchwork with straight seams than it is to set angle pieces into corners. People who intend to piece by machine are usually advised to select or adapt designs that can be sewn with straight seams, and those choices affect the graphic impact of the pattern.

Another technological change is that we now have polyester batting to take the place of the natural fibers. The synthetic batting is lighter and warmer than cotton. It holds together better, and requires far less quilting; thus the modern quiltmaker can design quilting patterns for specific graphic effects rather than having to put a line of quilting over every inch of surface whether the design requires one or not. (This also means that you have time to quilt by hand because there is so much less quilting to do.) The third great advantage of the new batting is that it requires no quilting frame. Quilts stuffed with cotton or wool were stretched very tightly during quilting, so that when the work was finished and the tension released, the batting would puff up between the lines of stitches. Polyester batting is much more resilient than cotton, and it puffs whether you stretch it or not.

SEWING BY HAND OR MACHINE

I usually do piecework on the machine because the seams in piecework will be hidden inside the quilt. As long as the stitching is strong and even, it makes no earthly difference whether it was sewn by hand or machine. But piecework can of course be done by hand as well (though not as quickly) if you prefer, and you may prefer to do it that way if you are going to carry the work around with you.

I do most appliqué by hand, using invisible whip stitches, because I think it looks better. It is certainly possible to appliqué by machine, using a straight topstitch, zigzag, or satin stitch. The effect is more informal and more insistently contemporary than invisible hand appliqué.

I also prefer to quilt by hand because quilting is visible and I think the traditional technique looks better. It is possible to quilt small things on the sewing machine, and we often do pillow tops or baby quilts that way. But for a large piece, machine quilting is really more trouble than it's worth. Since it is difficult to turn a huge quilt every few seconds to stitch around curves or corners, you are pretty well confined by the machine to a straight-line quilting pattern. So I don't like it.

18

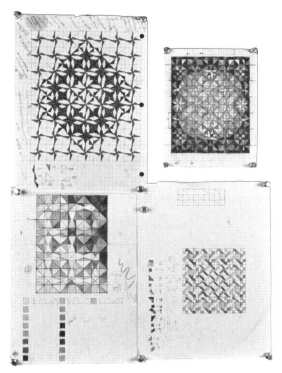

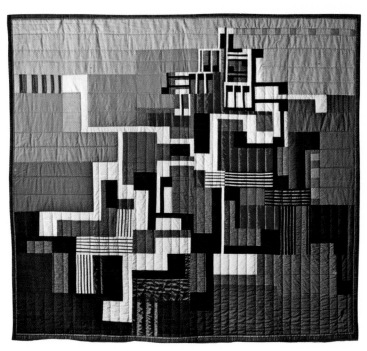

I. Working Drawings: *Frank and Nancy's Quilt* (upper left); *Night and Day* (lower left); *Wheels* (lower right); *Judy in Arabia* (upper right). Margin notes have to do with yardage and numbers of pieces needed.

II. *Note Motion* (91″ × 104″) by Molly Upton

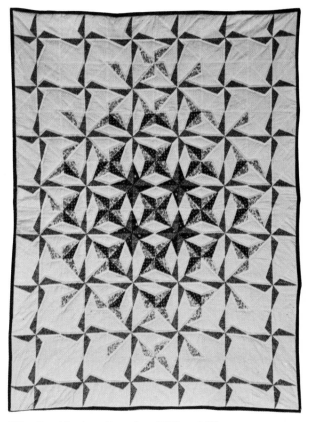

III. *Pace Victoria* (39″ × 50″) by Beth Gutcheon

IV. *Cynthia Ann Dancing* (62″ × 82″) by Beth Gutcheon

V. *Card Trick* (53″ × 53″) by Jeffrey Gutcheon. Notice that *Card Trick* and *Crow's Nest* are the same pattern colored differently.

VI. *Judy in Arabia* (66″ × 78″) by Jeffrey Gutcheon

VII. *Kaleidoscope* (105″ × 105″) by Beth Gutcheon

VIII. *Crow's Nest* (72″ × 88″) by Jeffrey Gutcheon

How to Use This Book

DESIGNING PATCHWORK

A piecework quilt design is usually composed of one or more *repeating design units.* The unit may be one single patch of a particular size and shape, as in the *Baby's Blocks* or *Grandmother's Flower Garden* patterns, composed entirely of diamonds or of hexagons (see p. 137). But the most characteristically American designs and the most versatile use more complex repeating *blocks.* The blocks, which are usually square (but not always), are individual designs that become the building blocks with which you construct larger overall patterns. They may be purely traditional ones handed down through generations, they may be modified versions of traditional ones, or they may be wholly original. You will find all three kinds here, and we hope that you will eventually be moved to devise your own.

The way blocks are arranged within the larger pattern is called the *set.* When you begin to dissect patchwork, you look first for the repeating design element—whether it is a one-patch, a block, or several blocks—and you then identify the *set,* or method by which the elements were joined to make a larger pattern. Outside the central design area there will sometimes be *borders,* either of plain fabric or in a design pieced in strips.

COLORING THE LINE DRAWINGS

As you can see from looking at the drawings and the color plates, a piecework design can be varied tremendously according to the way it is colored in. The number of colors you use and the way you position lights and darks can in fact make two versions of the same pattern appear to be totally different. For a sample, we have shown you a drawing of my quilt *Rolling Pinwheel* in line art on p. 22 and again in three different shadings on p. 23. You can see the way I colored it in plate XII, facing p. 146; notice that it is not quite the same as any of the black and white variations.

Before you actually begin to work, let me remind you that quiltmaking is a craft and that crafts are distinguished from industrial processes in that the design and the making of the piece are not separable. The way a piece is designed has everything to do with how it will be sewn, how long it will take, how hard it will be, and what techniques will be used. Or to start from the other end, the amount of time and skill you have and the techniques you want to use have much to do with the design you should choose. To design well you should have a grasp of the craft as a whole; so before you actually take pencil in hand, please read the general instructions all the way through.

First, look at the color plates in the book and get a feel for

3. Line drawing of *Rolling Pinwheel*

22

4. Three sample shadings of *Rolling Pinwheel*

23

what is possible. Compare the color plates to their corresponding line drawings. Then choose a design that interests you, put a piece of tracing paper over the drawing, and set to work with colored pencils.

In the drawings, dotted lines indicate seam lines. They are shown in dotted lines instead of solid ones when they are a necessary part of the construction but not necessarily part of the design. If the pieces on either side of the dotted line are the same color in your design, then the seam will show very little in the finished patchwork. If you choose to make the pieces different colors, the line will become distinct.

You can see a few of our working drawings in the color plate facing p. 18. The working drawing is a color code, not a finished composition. It shows how many colors you are using, whether they are light or dark, and how the lights and darks are arranged. But the pencil colors do not necessarily correspond to the fabric colors you will ultimately choose.

Start with one block in the pattern. Color it in a way that pleases you, then color all the surrounding blocks exactly the same way to see what larger patterns emerge. Try using two colors in the block, then four, then more. Try putting darks in certain areas, then color the next block with the lights where the darks were to get a positive-negative effect. Try developing two or more colorations for the block and alternate them in the same drawing to see what happens. Try changing the colors of certain blocks at random. If you are reaching for perspective effects, remember that bright intense colors project and light dim colors recede.

At first, the easiest thing to do well is a pattern in which each block is colored the same. That means few fabric choices and easier organization and faster cutting for you. So I recommend that for a beginner. You can of course use an assortment of scraps combined at random, as I have in *David's Quilt* (facing p. 147), or you can alter the shading through a wide range of gradations, as Jeffrey has done in *Judy in Arabia* (facing p. 19). Just remember that the more fabrics you use, the more difficult it becomes to control the materials and to produce exactly the effect you intend. Combining fabrics artfully is a skill that must be learned.

TRANSFORMING THE DESIGN INTO PATCHWORK

When you have finished the line drawing, you can, of course, simply frame it and give it to your mother for Christmas. But if you plan to make it into patchwork, we should back up a little and talk about some practical considerations in choosing a quilt pattern.

THE SIZE OF THE PROJECT

The length of time it will take you to cut and sew a patchwork pattern has very little to do with the quilt's size. What counts is the number of pieces in the pattern. With each pattern we have offered a set of guidelines so that if you make the quilt exactly as we have laid it out, it will have a certain number of pieces (which is counted out for you) and it will come out a certain size. If you want to make a king-size bedspread and the design you are looking at will only fit a double bed, you are either going to have to enlarge the design or choose a different one.

Here is the way I gauge projects. Anything with 400 to 700 pieces is a comfortable project, by which I mean it would probably take me about forty hours to make the quilt if I piece by machine and quilt by hand. From 700 to 1,000 pieces is a major effort suitable for ceremonial gifts to people you like very much, and anything over 1,000 is sheer punishment.

Granted, your tolerances may be quite different from mine. There's a lady named Grace Snyder in Nebraska who makes quilts with 94,000 pieces in them, and she sews them by hand. She thinks it's fun. She's about ninety-two. Once I was giving a seminar in Lincoln at the opening of a quilt show that included several of her quilts. I hoped to meet her at the opening but found that she had decided not to come. "Ah, poor dear," I thought, "she's too frail to travel." But not at all; I learned that she had chosen that week to visit her daughter in Florida. Don't let me scare you off a big project if you like the work and have the time.

THE DIFFICULTY OF THE PROJECT

The second consideration in choosing a pattern is its difficulty. This too has been rated for you on each pattern. I must say that none of these patterns are *very* hard to sew—not as hard as turning a lapel properly, for instance—so if you have some experience sewing, forget the ratings and make your own judgment. But if you have never sewn before, you can learn to sew patchwork perfectly well; in fact, I think it's the best kind of sewing to start on. But you wouldn't necessarily be able to guess ahead of time which patterns were trickier than others, so I've figured it out for you.

BED QUILT	TWIN 39" x 75"	DOUBLE 54" x 75"	QUEEN 60" x 80"	KING 72" x 80"	CALIF. KING 80" x 80"
THROW	40" x 70"	55" x 70"	60" x 75"	72" x 76"	80" x 80"
COVERLET	57" x 84"	72" x 84"	78" x 90"	90" x 90"	98" x 90"
SPREAD	72" x 104"	88" x 104"	94" x 108"	106" x 106"	110" x 110"

5. Chart of quilt sizes

In general, the easiest patterns are those that go together with all straight seams, and almost all of these do because we make designs with that in mind. Within that category there are some shapes that give a little trouble in *laying up*. (By laying up, I mean the way you arrange two pieces, right sides together, before you sew them to each other.) I'll explain how to cope with laying up in the general sewing instructions, and in every pattern that might be tricky I've made a note in the step-by-step directions. Along with each pattern you will find a "piecing chart," a block from the pattern with the pieces numbered so you can see in what order they go together most easily. In many cases it will be so obvious that the piecing chart will insult your intelligence, but I hope you'll overlook that; I thought too much information would be better than too little. These piecing-chart blocks are also helpful because sometimes it is hard to be sure where the block is in a pattern, and this way you will have it right before you, nicely out of context.

ABOUT THE SIZE OF THE PATTERN

When you are deciding what size you want your quilt to be when it is finished, the first thing to consider is how the piece will be used. If you are going to hang it on the wall, you can be pretty flexible, but if you plan to use it on a bed, you must accept some limitations.

On the chart on p. 26 we have worked out a series of useful dimensions for different bed types and different quilt types. Along the top of the chart you see the name of the bed size, plus the dimensions of the top of the mattress. At the side you see the three most common kinds of quilt. You might also keep in mind that quilt batting comes precut in the following sizes: 72″ × 90″, 81″ × 96″, and 90″ × 108″.

A *throw* or lap quilt is small. It is made to be folded over the back of a sofa, ready to cover a napping body, or to tuck under your knees when you go for a drive in the surrey, or to be folded at the foot of a bed during the day and pulled up for warmth at night. It is usually about the size of the top of the mattress, without much drop.

A *coverlet* covers the top of the bed, with a 7″ to 9″ drop on both sides and the end. That means it will cover the mattress sides and end, but it will not go over the pillows and it will not cover the box spring if any. In a formal bedroom a person might make a matching pillow sham and dust ruffle to go with the coverlet if it is to be the bed's daytime covering.

A full *spread* covers the pillows and box spring. I would say it reaches to the floor except I don't know how long the legs of your bed are. Box springs and mattresses are usually 7″ deep, so if you want the spread to cover them, you add 15″ to 17″ on sides and end. If you want the spread to cover the pillows, you add another 12″ at the top. I am telling you this so you will understand how the standard sizes are arrived at and will feel free to change them if they don't apply to your needs.

CHANGING THE SIZE OF THE QUILT

There are several ways to make a quilt larger. One is to add more patchwork units to the design. Another is to keep the number of units the same but to make each one larger. A third is to add borders to the existing design. To make a design smaller, you reverse these processes: Remove a row of blocks, make all the blocks smaller, or eliminate borders.

WHEN TO ADD MORE BLOCKS

If a quilt is five rows of blocks wide and seven rows long, you can obviously make it larger by making the pattern six rows by seven or six rows by eight, ad infinitum. The principal thing to consider is that each row of blocks you add increases the number of pieces you must cut out and sew together. If the quilt has a pieced border, remember also to figure in the extra border elements you will need to correspond to each new row of blocks. See p. 25 for a rule of thumb about how many pieces are too many. I usually choose to add more blocks to enlarge a quilt when the total number of pieces in the revised design will be fewer than 750.

WHEN TO ALTER THE SCALE

You will notice that several designs in this book have a specific proportion that is determined by the design. For instance, *Kaleidoscope* (facing p. 19) and *The Star Also Rises* (facing p. 146) are square. They can be 60″ square or 120″ square, but they should not be turned into rectangles. Similarly, both *Judy in Arabia* (facing p. 19) and *Cynthia Ann Dancing* (facing p. 18) have to be made in a certain number of rows, so that the color scheme will be properly centered. For such patterns I usually prefer either to change the scale of the pattern or to put on extra borders rather than to add blocks.

Also if the patchwork design already has 600 to 700 pieces

in it, but the finished size of the quilt must be larger, I would make the blocks larger rather than add more piecework. When you like the pattern but feel it has too many pieces, you can make the blocks larger and eliminate one row or more to bring the piece count down. And sometimes you may want to alter the scale in the other direction. If you feel a pattern is really too overblown to be interesting or that it would benefit from being more intense, make the blocks smaller and add another row of them.

If you decide to change the scale of the blocks, consider the following: If you make the block so small that any of the pieces in it are smaller than about 2″ square, you are letting yourself in for some pretty finicky cutting. If you are a beginner, you might find the tiny pieces hard to sew and hard to quilt. On the other end of the scale, I wouldn't make a block larger than about 20″ square unless the entire quilt were to be enormous and, further to be seen in a large room. The very large scale would be overpowering or simply boring unless it were done in a very calculated way for a specific effect.

I usually use blocks 8″ to 10″ square for a baby's quilt or small throw, and for anything larger I prefer 12″ to 16″ blocks, depending on the complexity of the block and the finished size of the piece. The size of the block will be partly determined by its internal organization. For instance, *Rolling Pinwheel* is a four-patch, but each of its four quadrants is divided into three equal dimensions on each side. If I make the block 12″ square, each of these internal units will measure 2″. If I make it 15″ square, each of the internal units will measure 2½″. But if I make it 14″ square, each of the internal divisions will measure 2⅓″. Standard rulers do not have thirds of inches measured on them, so we have given you an inch divided into thirds for you to trace out and use to make your own measuring device if necessary. But obviously you save yourself some trouble if you choose a multiple of three for the outside measurements of a block divided in this way, just as it would be easier to use a multiple of four for a block that falls on a grid of four equal modules.

WHEN TO ADD BORDERS

A very good way to fill out the dimensions of the pattern you have chosen is to add one or more wide plain border strips. A quilt on a bed is not seen as a whole surface, the way you see a painting on a wall or, for that matter, the way you see your design on paper. Quilts are often designed so that the main

8a. Drawing the block full size on graph paper

8b. Full-size block plus border unit; X on each shape needed for template

8c. Cutting out (shaded) template pieces

30

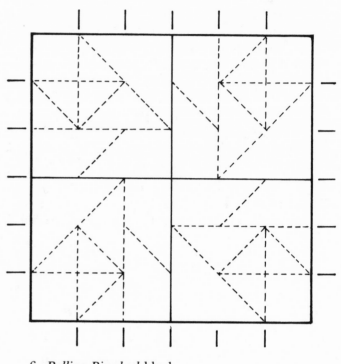

6. *Rolling Pinwheel* block

7. An inch divided into thirds

pattern is roughly the size of the top of the mattress and the drops at the sides of the bed are composed of borders. These borders act as the frame for the design and can do a great deal to define it and set it off properly. For example, it is often effective to have the innermost border be a narrow strip matching the background of the patchwork; this creates the impression that the foreground of the patchwork is floating on a larger field of background material. Outside that add one or more contrasting strips, each somewhat wider than the last. These might be made of some fabric that also appears in the patchwork, or you might choose a solid color corresponding to some print in the patchwork, or you might choose something entirely different to complete the color spectrum for the composition as a whole.

MAKING TEMPLATES

When you have determined the size of the blocks, the next step is to make templates, or cutting patterns. You need a template for each piece of a given size and shape in the pattern. It is important that the templates be made very accurately, for every small error in them is multiplied many times when you use it to cut many pieces, and in the end such mistakes make the sewing difficult or impossible. The safest and easiest way is to draw the whole block to size on graph paper, then cut out the pieces you need. If the quilt has a pieced border, draw a unit of it to size along with the block. If you were making *Rolling Pinwheel* with 15″ blocks, you would take a large sheet of graph paper, which you can buy at an art-supply store (or architect or engineer's supply store), and actually draw the whole *Rolling Pinwheel* block on it, 15″ square. If you can't get big graph paper, buy a graph paper pad and tape several sheets together, to the size you need. (Be very careful to match up the lines in both directions so the graph will be consistent over the entire area.) You need those straight lines and right angles to be sure your drawing is accurate.

TEMPLATES FOR MACHINE SEWING

When you have very carefully cut out the pieces you need, tape or glue them to a piece of poster board, leaving at least ½″ between them. (You can get poster board at any stationery store or art-supply store.) Or you can use any strong, thin cardboard. Measure a line all around the outside of each piece *exactly* paral-

31

9a. Taping template shapes to poster board

9b. Measuring dots ¼″ from paper edge

9c. Connecting the dots using a dressmaker's T-square

32

lel to the edge of the paper shape and *exactly* ¼″ from it. This is the seam margin, and it must be made very, very accurately.

Calculate the seam margins by using a ruler perpendicular to the paper edge and drawing a series of dots ¼″ from the seam. Then connect these dots with the long edge of the ruler. Or if you can find one, use a dressmaker's T square, an inexpensive and invaluable instrument of thin clear plastic printed with a grid for drawing perfect parallels.

One more note about seam margins. A ¼″ margin is good because it is wide enough for safety but not so wide as to leave a lot of waste fabric inside the quilt to interfere with quilting. But for beginning sewers I sometimes recommend ⅜″ just to be safe. A wider margin gives you more room for error if your sewing is uncertain and your seams wobbly. It doesn't really matter which you choose as long as you draw the margins accurately and use the same margin width throughout.

TEMPLATES FOR HAND SEWING

When you make templates for hand sewing, you do not add seam margins. Instead, paste the graph paper to poster board and cut out a template the size of the finished piece. When you trace for cutting, you will leave a space ½″ wide or more between each piece. Then cut, making a ¼″ seam margin by eye around the outside of the traced line. That way you will have the correct sewing line right on the fabric to guide you.

CALCULATING THE CUTTING

When all the templates are made, figure out how many pieces you need in each color and mark the number on the appropriate template. (Naturally, you can't do this if you are making a scrap quilt or one with a great variety of fabrics in a nonrepeating pattern.) Keep in mind that the colors on your line drawing are essentially a color code rather than a literal rendering of the colors of the finished piece, because you may not be able to get the exact shades of each color you want.

You can calculate the amount of fabric you need mathematically with what my husband calls "a little simple trigonometry." Personally I prefer to work it out empirically. I start by assuming that the fabric will be 45″ wide, because it almost always is these days. (If you find yourself with fabric 36″ wide, remember to buy extra.) Let's say I'm calculating fabric needs for *Rolling Pinwheel.* I see that I need forty-eight of the small yellow triangles. So I take the template for that piece, and I test to see how many will fit in a row across fabric 45″ wide. Then I figure out how many rows I will need to get forty-eight pieces. I multiply the number of rows by the height of the rows, and I add a couple of inches for each row just to be safe. If you are using machine-sewing templates, fit them flush together as tightly as you can. But if you are sewing by hand remember to leave *at least* ½″ between each template when figuring how many you can cut from a row.

You should work out exactly how much fabric you need as closely as you can before you go to the fabric store. If you can, buy extra; you will always be able to use it in a scrap quilt someday, or for patches or pot holders or Christmas tree ornaments. But sometimes you can't buy extra, either because you have your heart set on some imported fabric at seven dollars a yard or because the piece you want is a remnant and three quarters of a yard is all there is. At that point, you must know exactly how little you can get away with.

CHOOSING FABRIC FOR PATCHWORK

Traditionally, patchwork quilts have nearly always been made out of dress-weight cotton or homespun. It is inexpensive, easy to sew, washes well, and is light enough to quilt. (Picture the fact that the quilting needle has to weave in and out of the three-layered quilt. If the fabrics are too heavy, the needle will bend or break.) That said, I must admit that if you are not interested in washing or quilting your quilt, that is, if you don't mind dry cleaning and you will be content to secure the three layers with knots, then you can use any fabric you like. I don't recommend knits because they are stretchy and hard to piece well, but some quiltmakers use them. Silks and velvets are hard to work with because they are fragile and slippery and sometimes show pinholes; but again, if you know what you're getting into, it's fine to use them. They add texture and luster to patchwork and give the quilt a luxurious gloss.

If you do plan to use traditional cotton fabrics, the first thing you will discover is that you can hardly find cotton. This is too bad, because cotton is easier to work with than the blends or synthetics. It has both body and give, which is important when you are forcing pieces to fit exactly and they don't quite want to. But the most important thing to consider is whether you like the color and print of the fabric. If the one you love is 80-percent polyester, buy it anyway, but when you have a choice, opt for the fabric with the highest cotton content.

Be flexible about colors. Choosing fabrics for patchwork is

not the same as choosing fabrics to wear or to upholster your couch. Remember that it is the total effect of the fabrics together in your quilt that will matter, not any one individual fabric. Try to vary the size and shape of the prints you use; don't use only tiny flowers or middle-size paisleys or thin stripes. When choosing large-scale prints, consider carefully how they will look cut into small pieces. Try not to have all the colors in the same intensity range (the same degree of lightness or darkness).

One of the challenges of patchwork is that you cannot totally control your palette the way a painter can. You may see in your mind exactly what shade you want to use, but you just can't find it in fabric. Be prepared to compromise. Try to shop with as open a mind as possible; refer to your colored design, which tells you how many colors you need but not *which* colors they are. Be prepared to go out with a design in red, green, and brown and to come home with fabrics in maroon, navy, and orange if that's what worked best. Try not to buy one fabric until you have chosen them all, held them at arm's length, and squinted at them (to compare their intensity) or until you have stood twenty feet away from them to see what impact they have from across the room.

When I have done all this, I go home and test each fabric for colorfastness. (Dip a scrap in warm water, then lay it on a white paper towel to see if the color runs.) Then I wash and dry the fabrics together to be sure they are all preshrunk, no matter what the manufacturer claims. There are those who don't bother with this, and ninety percent of the time it won't make any difference, but I have nightmares about having one color run onto the white background or about having one fabric shrink when none of the others do after the quilt is finished.

And then, if you have the heart, you should cut out one block and sew it up, tack it on the wall, and stand across the room from it to be sure that you like what you've chosen. Sometimes you find that that little green print looks white from a distance and throws your whole scheme out of balance. But other times you will have a deep-seated irrational conviction that however it comes out you're going to love it, and whenever that feeling comes over me, I follow it blindly and forget about the test block.

TRACING AND CUTTING

If you are sewing by hand, you have made templates that have no seam margins. This is because you want the tracing line to be your sewing line as well. You have to trace out each piece one at a time on the wrong side of the fabric, using a sharp pencil. Be careful not to drag too hard on the pencil, making the fabric slip under the template. If you have very dark fabrics in your quilt and have trouble seeing the pencil line on them, use a chalk pencil and make your templates out of sandpaper, which will grip the fabric and prevent slipping.

You may find that a colored pencil works better than graphite for tracing hand-sewing work, but be sure you test to see what happens to the colored marks when the fabrics are ironed. Some such pencils have a wax base that will set right onto the patchwork, and you'll never get it out. If it passes the hot iron test, see what happens when you wash and dry it. *Do not use ink markers for hand-sewing work.*

If you are going to sew by machine, then you have made templates with seam margins already added, and the line you mark onto the fabric is the cutting line, not the sewing line. For dressmaking, guiding marks from ⅜″ to ⅝″ from the needle are usually engraved on the throat plate, but the ¼″ seam is the easiest of all because you simply use the outside of the presser foot as a guide.

Since the line you trace is the cutting line and since there need be no sewing line actually on the piece, you can cut more than one piece out at a time as long as you baste *very* carefully and make sure the cutting is accurate. Notice also that if you are going to cut several layers at a time, there will be some fabric wasted, so be sure you have enough before you start cutting.

The good old-fashioned method of tracing and cutting each piece one by one is without doubt the most accurate and the most economical, but not all of us like it. So when you have to cut large numbers of regular shapes, you can proceed in the following manner:

Suppose I am cutting the little white squares for *Rolling Pinwheel.* I need 116 squares for blocks and border. I can fit 14 in one row across the fabric; 8 × 14 = 112, so if I cut out eight rows at one time, I will just need to cut out 4 more squares. Working on an ironing board, I fold one double row as shown. I carefully match the selvedges, and I make sure I have left plenty of leeway at top and bottom; then I press the crease with a hot steam iron. Then I roll the row over six more times pressing in the creases each time. This will result in a flattened tube eight layers thick. We have found that with care we can cut as many as eight layers accurately, but not more.

If the folds have been made tight and smooth, the inside

10a. Folded fabric being creased

10b. Tracing the template on top layer

10c. Pinning at each corner

10d. Cutting all layers

11. Cutting ¼″ outside the line after fabric is marked for hand sewing

12a. Fabric wrong side up, template wrong side up; piece comes out correct

12b. Fabric wrong side up, template right side up; piece comes out wrong

layers should be nearly the same size as those outside, though in the nature of things the inside must be slightly smaller. Keep this in mind when you trace. Center the template as much as possible between top and bottom of the row.

To trace, use a washable-ink nylon-tip marker. This is better than pencil because it doesn't get dull and it is easy to make a line you can see without exerting pressure. What ink remains on the fabric after cutting will wash out easily without setting on the quilt top. (Don't use an indelible marker; if it doesn't wash out, it may be visible inside the work, and more likely it will run lightly onto the quilt top and set forever.)

Trace the row of squares onto the top layer of the flattened tube, as shown. Make thin, light ink marks, then put straight pins in every corner of each shape, as shown, to baste it together. It is at the corners that the layers start to shift during cutting, and if that happens, the shapes will all be slightly different and when you start to sew you will be very unhappy.

Cut with good, sharp fabric shears. Fabric shears should have blades of forged steel and should never be used on paper or in fact on anything but fabric.

Cut one at a time when you only have a few of one shape to cut out, or when you are not absolutely sure that you have extra fabric (because you lose an inch or two with each fold, and if you try to skimp, you may wind up with a whole row that is incomplete).

NONREVERSIBLE PIECES
(MIRROR IMAGES)

Cut one at a time when the shape is not the same on the front as on the back. Look, for example, at the trapezoids that make up the center pinwheel in *Rolling Pinwheel*. Those shapes are not reversible; they have a right side, which is up, and a wrong side down. If you cut with the right side of the template on the wrong side of the fabric, you will get a mirror image of the shape you need. If the fabric is the same on both sides, it will make no difference, but if it is not, you must be careful to have the wrong side up on the wrong side of the fabric so the right side will be the right way up. If you cut many layers as described above, every other row would come out wrong because every other layer of fabric would be the wrong way up.

If you greatly prefer to cut these shapes many at a time, measure and cut the fabric into strips wide enough for a row. Lay them one on top of the next, wrong sides up. Then trace, pin, and cut.

SEWING BY HAND

Along with each pattern there is a piecing chart telling you the best order in which to assemble the pieces for each block. Lay the first two pieces right sides together, matching the penciled sewing lines carefully; secure with pins. Use pure cotton thread (polyester thread knots) or use quilting thread if you can get it. Quilting thread is coated with silicone to prevent knotting. If you can't get it, buy a lump of beeswax at any notions store and coat the cotton thread with it each time you thread the needle. (Again, this is to prevent the thread from tying itself in knots while you are sewing.) Use size 8 sharp needles (size 7 or 9 will do) and make an honest effort to learn to use a thimble; you will definitely need it for quilting, so you might as well start now. The thimble goes on the third finger of the sewing hand. You use it to push the needle through the fabric. Secure the beginning of the line of sewing with a knot or backstitch (your choice). Take three or four running stitches as small and even as you can manage on your needle at one time. Push the needle through with the thimble, pull it out with your thumb and index finger, and take a backstitch for strength. Check the back of the sewing to be sure the seam is going through the sewing line on both sides. Sew to the end of the seam with combined running stitches and backstitches, as described, and secure with a knot or backstitch at the end of the seam. Unless you are setting in a corner, and you won't be unless there is a special note to that effect, you can sew right to the edge of the fabric and you probably should.

It's best to press each seam before you sew another seam across it, but sometimes you will be carrying your work somewhere where there is no iron; in that case, press the work flat with your fingers as best you can.

SEWING BY MACHINE

Use a size 14 needle and any good sewing thread; polyester is fine for machine sewing. You can use one color thread throughout. About eight or ten stitches to the inch is strong but flexible. Sew one block together, following the piecing chart. For the *Rolling Pinwheel* block the process would go like this:

First, notice that the block is divided into four identical quadrants. If you do each step I describe four times (4×), you will finish the whole block at the same moment.

Sew 1 to 2. There is no need to baste them; just lay them together with edges matching and run them through the machine, guiding the raw edges against the presser foot to get a

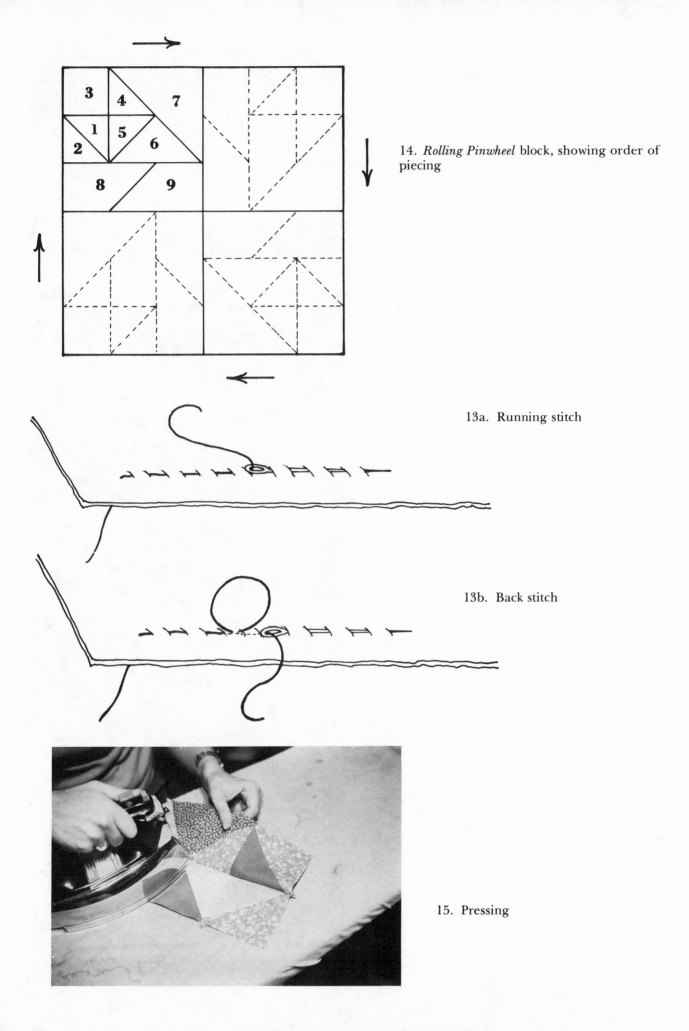

14. *Rolling Pinwheel* block, showing order of piecing

13a. Running stitch

13b. Back stitch

15. Pressing

16. Basted joint being sewn on machine

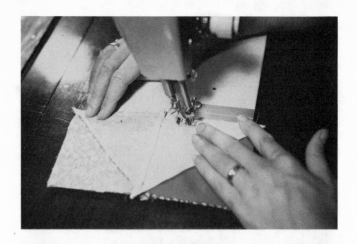

17a. Patchwork basted at joints, refusing to fit

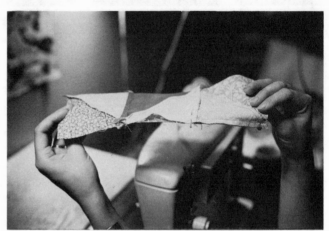

17b. Shirring between the joints takes up the slack evenly

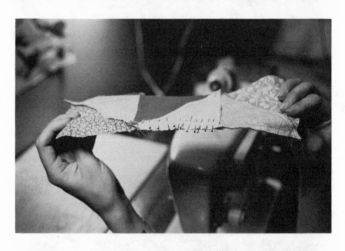

17c. Sewing over the shirring pins

perfect ¼″ margin. (If you prefer, you can place a piece of masking tape on the throat plate parallel to the seam line and exactly ¼″ from the needle and use that for a seam guide.) There is no need to knot or backstitch; each seam will be locked by the next seam crossing it.

PRESSING

After each piece has been sewn, it should be pressed crisp and flat before it is sewn to the next piece so there will be no chance of sewing in any rolls or puckers. Press from the top with a hot iron, with steam if possible. Use the hottest temperature you can for the fiber content of your fabrics. (If you are using certain synthetics or blends, be careful not to melt them.) Press on top of the work, having the seam margins underneath fall together to one side of the seam, preferably toward the darker fabric so they won't show through the top. You don't want the margins pressed open. They are too narrow, you would burn your fingers, and it interferes with quilting later on.

Sew 1–2 to 3. Press. Sew 4 to 5. Press. Sew 4–5 to 6. Press.

BASTING THE JOINTS

The next step is to sew 1–2–3 to 4–5–6. The seam line between 1 and 3 should exactly meet the seam line between 4 and 5. I call this the joint for lack of a better word. The joints must be made perfectly because patchwork is a sort of graphic design, and in order for the graphics to work, the lines must meet perfectly as if they were pencil lines on paper. Lay the pieces right sides together, with the seams matching, and baste with a pin right in the seam, as shown. Leave the pin in place till the new seam is completed. Most machines will just slip over the pin, but if worse comes to worst, you may break a needle once in a while. Never mind it. (It won't hurt the machine.)

Sometimes you will have to stretch the patchwork to make all the joints meet perfectly, especially when you are in the final stages of the piecing because by then all your tiny cumulative errors have caught up with you. That's when you will be glad of cotton fabric because it can be stretched. Shir the pieces to make them fit, and if you have to, sew in a pucker before you let the joints miss each other. When the batting is in place, a little pucker is barely noticeable, but if the lines of the pattern don't meet up, you can see it across the room.

18a. Trapezoids **8** and **9** facing each other

18b. If you lay them up with edges matching . . .

18c. they will come out off-center.

44

18d. Instead, baste them off-center with a fake seam of pins . . .

18e. then open out to see if they are right.

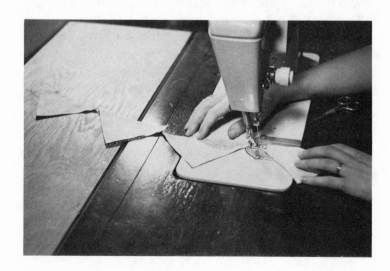

19. Chain of piecing

45

TEST-BASTING A LAY-UP

The next step is to sew 8 to 9. As you can see from the photograph, if you lay up the pieces with their edges matching, the piece will be off-center when you open the work after sewing. The pieces must be laid up off-center, as shown. You will soon get the hang of this, but in any case where you are unsure, it is best to test-baste with a quick, fake seam of pins where the sewn seam will fall (see photo). Open the work out; if it is not exactly right, remove the pins, adjust the lay-up, and try again. When you have it right, sew the seam and keep that piece as a guide for laying up the rest of the similar pieces in the quilt.

Here is an alternate method of perfecting the lay-up of difficult pieces: With pencil and ruler, find and draw the actual seam lines on the back of the pieces you want to lay up. Use the technique shown on p. 32 to find a line ¼″ in from the raw edge of the fabric. Put the pieces right sides together and impale the two in such a way that the pin goes through the two corners front and back exactly. Pin the rest of the seam, sew, and use this piece as a guide for laying up the others.

To finish the quadrant, sew 7 to 4–6. Press. Sew 1–2–3–4–5–6–7 to 8–9. Press. Repeat for other three quadrants.

ASSEMBLY-LINE PIECING

Once you have made one block, you can either finish the whole quilt by making block after block just as you began or you can break down the process into an assembly line. The latter is far faster and more methodical, though less organic. Here's how it goes:

Take all the number 1 pieces for the whole quilt and sew them to all the number 2 pieces. Don't stop to clip the threads or to press; just feed them into the machine one after the other. You don't even have to lift the presser foot or pull the pieces out behind. When you are done, you will have a long chain of patchwork, and you can then clip and press with much less wasted motion. Do the same for each succeeding step, completing each one for all the blocks in the quilt. In this way you will finish all the blocks at the same time. Then you simply join them into horizontal rows, sew the rows together, and you are done. Cut or piece the borders in strips and add them, taking care to baste all joints. When adding plain border strips, be sure to baste them thoroughly, with a pin at least every 3″, or the long strips will stretch. (Believe me.)

MARKING ON THE QUILTING DESIGN

The next step is to choose a quilting design and to mark it onto the top before the three layers are assembled. The quilting pattern you choose depends largely on your taste and on how much time you have. Try not to leave areas more than about 8″ square with no quilting at all because the batting may shred and lump if it isn't secured well enough.

Mark the pattern you have chosen directly on the quilt top with light pencil lines or with chalk pencil. You can make straight lines with a yardstick or a chalked string snapped across the quilt, and you can make other shapes by tracing around household objects such as teacups and dinner plates. Make larger arcs with a string-and-pencil compass. Tie a string around a pencil, hold the end of the string where you want the center of the circle to be, then draw the arc, keeping the pencil vertical and the string taut. Or you can use commercial templates (see p. 167 for where to order them) or you can make your own templates. Draw whatever shape you like on poster board or trace shapes out of books, coloring books, or from old quilts. If you want the design larger or smaller, you can have a photostat copy made in any size you need for about two dollars.

Transfer the shape to poster board with carbon paper. I don't recommend using dressmaker's carbon paper to transfer a drawing directly onto the top because it is hard to center the pattern perfectly with carbon paper obscuring the patchwork. Also, you might have to wash the quilt to remove the traces of marking, while with a light pencil line the mark seems to disappear after the quilting is in place. (If you look closely you often find faint pencil markings on antique quilts that have never been washed.)

PIECING THE BACKING

After the top is marked and pressed (this is the last chance you will have to take an iron to it), piece a sheet of backing the same size as the top or a bit larger. The traditional backing is unbleached muslin, either in pure cotton or cotton polyester blend. If you use pure cotton, be sure to wash and iron it well to preshrink, even if it claims to be preshrunk. You can, of course, use colored or printed fabrics instead of off-white; but I find that the quilting stitches on the underside of the quilt tend to look much less even than the top ones, and they show up least if the backing matches the quilting thread. If you're a very good quilter, or not vain, or if you're using a dark quilting thread, feel free to use dark backing. One more caveat: You will often find ladies' magazines gaily urging you to use a bed sheet for quilt backing because it's high-quality fabric and it's already the size of a bed. This turns out to be a bad idea unless you can find some bad sheets. Good percale sheets are very tightly woven, with many more threads to the inch than dime-store muslin, and they are consequently difficult to quilt. Your needle sticks and squeaks every inch of the way, and it slows you down and sets your teeth on edge.

Unless the quilt is for a fancy gift or for sale for a high price, I wouldn't worry about where the seams fall on the backing. I usually piece backing in horizontal strips. Traditional quilts are often backed with odd-size scraps of homespun with irregular seams all over the place.

ADDING THE BATTING

Lay the backing out on a clean bare floor, wrong side up. Carefully unroll a polyester quilt bat over the backing, being sure not to stretch or tear it. Try to center the two layers, and carefully smooth out any lumps or wrinkles. You can buy batting at fabric or notions stores, or order it by mail (see p. 168). Be sure whatever batting you use is densely made in a cohesive sheet. If it is loose, like pillow filling, it will need as much quilting as cotton batting, and it may even work its way out of the top between the seams in later years. If you decide to use cotton batting for any reason, either quilt it so that a line of stitching falls *at least* every two inches or vow never to have the quilt washed. If you want to do little or no quilting, use a light, washable blanket as filler or back the quilt with that prequilted fabric they sell for making bathrobes.

PIECED BATTING

Standard batting comes in sizes 72″ × 90″, 81″ × 96″, and 90″ × 108″. Whenever possible, you should buy batting larger than the size of your quilt top and trim it to fit. You should never try to assemble a bat out of many small pieces because there is every likelihood that the pieces will come apart inside the quilt later on and you will have to take the whole thing apart and start over. But once in a while you will have a quilt that is longer or wider than the largest quilt bat, and you will have to add a piece of batting to fill out the necessary dimension. With bonded or tightly finished polyester batting you can overlap the two edges to be joined and sew them very slowly on the machine with a wide zigzag stitch. This will compress the batting slightly so the ridge made by the double thickness of batting is scarcely noticeable. If necessary you could use a long machine straight stitch, although the second best choice is probably to zigzag or catch-stitch by hand. Remember to overlap, because this will leave less of a lump than a conventional right-sides-together seam.

When the batting is in place, spread the top over the batting, right side up. Center it and smooth out all wrinkles. Now start from one end and pin-baste the three layers together. Work only from the top of the quilt; if you try to keep a hand underneath, you will disarrange the layers. Use lots of sharp pins that will not rust. (Sometimes pins make little brown spots on the fabric, especially if you leave them in place a long while.) Work across the quilt row after row until you reach the other side. If you prefer you can start in the middle and work out equally in all directions. But you must not start at one end with a friend simultaneously beginning at the other; then you will end with a clump of shifted fabric in the middle.

If you are quilting in a frame or if you will not be hefting the work around very much, this pin-basting will be sufficient. If you are going to use a quilting hoop or to be carrying the work around a lot, rolling and unrolling it, you should add grids of thread-basting to the pinning. A grid 8" to 10" wide should be enough.

ABOUT FRAMES AND HOOPS

As I have said before, if you are using polyester batting and if you have basted the layers evenly and well, it really makes no difference if you use a frame or not. I use one if I'm at home because I happen to have one and because my husband often quilts with me (or I with him). A frame is very handy for holding the work in place for two or more people.

A frame, as the name implies, is a large rectangular brace that holds the quilt taut. Fabric is tacked to its wooden stretchers, and the quilt ends are in turn pinned or sewn to the fabric.

A quilting hoop is an oval-shaped lap frame much like a large embroidery hoop. It holds only a portion of the quilt taut at one time, so when you finish quilting one area you must take the hoop off and squeeze it on somewhere else. This could cause the three layers of the quilt to shift, so a quilt that is to be worked on a hoop must be thread-basted with a large grid of temporary stitches in addition to the pin-basting with which you originally secure the layers. The hoop's advantage over a frame is that it is portable, and that you can turn the hoop—

and thus, the work—around. This is a great help when the line you are stitching turns a corner and goes off in an awkward direction.

QUILTING WITHOUT A FRAME

I like quilting without a frame, although it is a little informal. I roll the quilt top up, lengthwise. Then I sit cross-legged on the floor or on my bed with about a 12″ section of quilt unrolled in my lap. I secure the work by attaching it with pins to the knees of my trousers. When I have finished the area in my lap, I unpin and slide the roll sideways like a typewriter carriage. I work row after row in this fashion until I reach the middle. Then I roll up the finished half, turn the work around, and work from the middle out to the other edge, rolling up the finished work as I go. It's nice, because wherever I stop working, I just roll up the quilt and put it away.

If you aren't comfortable sitting cross-legged, you can achieve the same effect by sitting in a chair with the rolled-up work before you on a table or ironing board and the section you are working on stretching down into your lap.

QUILTING BY HAND

A quilting stitch is a simple running stitch. You try to make the stitches as small and even as you can, but when you are just learning, even counts more than small. Cotton or wool batting, which was used in the old days, becomes very heavy when wet and dries slowly, putting the quilting stitches under great strain. If the stitches were not very small and even, the weight of the waterlogged material might well snap them. But polyester batting dries quickly on the line or in a dryer, and your stitches are going to hold up fine unless they're so loose that they snag on something.

Use a number 8 quilter's needle (also called a "between"). It's shorter than a "sharp," so it's less likely to bend or break. Use quilting thread if you can get it, and if not, use cotton thread coated with beeswax. Cut (don't bite or tear) a thread about 20″ long. Longer than that will knot. Thread the needle single and tie a single knot at the bottom of the thread. Starting at a point on a quilting line about a foot away from you, bring the needle up from the back to the top. Tug gently on the needle till you feel the knot pop through the backing. You want the knot to lodge in the batting, not to come flying out the top. Take small, even running stitches through all three layers of

50

21a. Take 3 or 4 even stitches; use thimble to push needle through

21b. Free hand underneath the work

21c. Back-lit photograph shows hands working together

20. Cutaway of quilting

clip

clip

fabric. I aim to take about eight stitches to the inch (i.e., four stitches on top and four spaces between them).

Most quilters find it easiest to work toward themselves or from right to left. When the quilting line takes a turn in an awkward direction, they simply end off and begin a new thread from a more comfortable angle. While quilting, keep your free hand under the work, and each time the needle comes through to the underside, its tip should graze your finger so that you know you have gone through all three layers. Pockmarked left-hand fingertips become the sign by which quilters know each other, like the secret handshake of the Elks. Just be careful not to stab yourself; it is Not Done to bleed on the backing. (If it should happen, dab the blood off quickly with cold water.) If you find the needle sticking, as it sometimes does in hot weather (or if you have made the mistake of including sheeting in your patchwork), dust your fingers with talcum powder.

To end off a line of quilting, tie a knot about ¼″ above the surface of the work. Slide the needle into the batting (not all the way through the back) and bring it out the top again, still following the quilting line, so that the long tail of thread inside will be caught by the next line of stitching. Give a light tug and the knot will disappear into the batting. You will notice that all this knot tugging is cleverly planned so that no one can tell where your stitching began or ended. This is very important to the quilting judges at the county fair, but I think it is equally important that your quilting not come out in the wash. I often add a backstitch at the beginning and end of the row, especially if the knot pops in and out too easily, and let the judges cluck their tongues. You can learn to do the backstitch so that it's almost undetectable.

MACHINE QUILTING

If you baste the three layers *very* thoroughly, you can quilt them on the sewing machine. This is easiest on small items that can be rotated easily, but you can machine-quilt a large quilt if you use a pattern that requires no turning, such as a grid or diagonal parallel lines. Use a long stitch, six to eight stitches to the inch, and a number 14 needle, unless there are fabrics as heavy as corduroy or velveteen in the top, in which case use a number 16 needle. Use transparent nylon thread on the spool, but keep regular cotton or polyester sewing thread in the bobbin. Nylon thread in the bobbin tends to get snarly, and it breaks a lot. Transparent thread on top allows the quilting to look as much as possible like handwork.

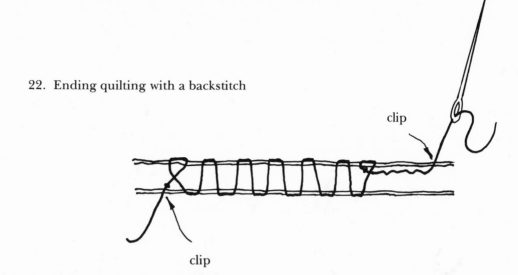

22. Ending quilting with a backstitch

clip

clip

23. Binding strip pinned through all layers

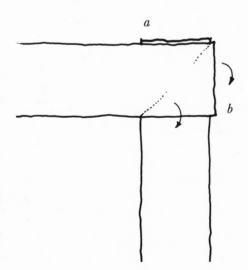

a

b

24a. Corner *b* is turned under to meet corner *a*

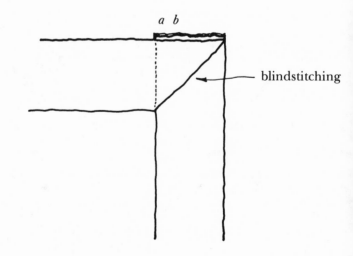

a b

blindstitching

24b. The mitred corner

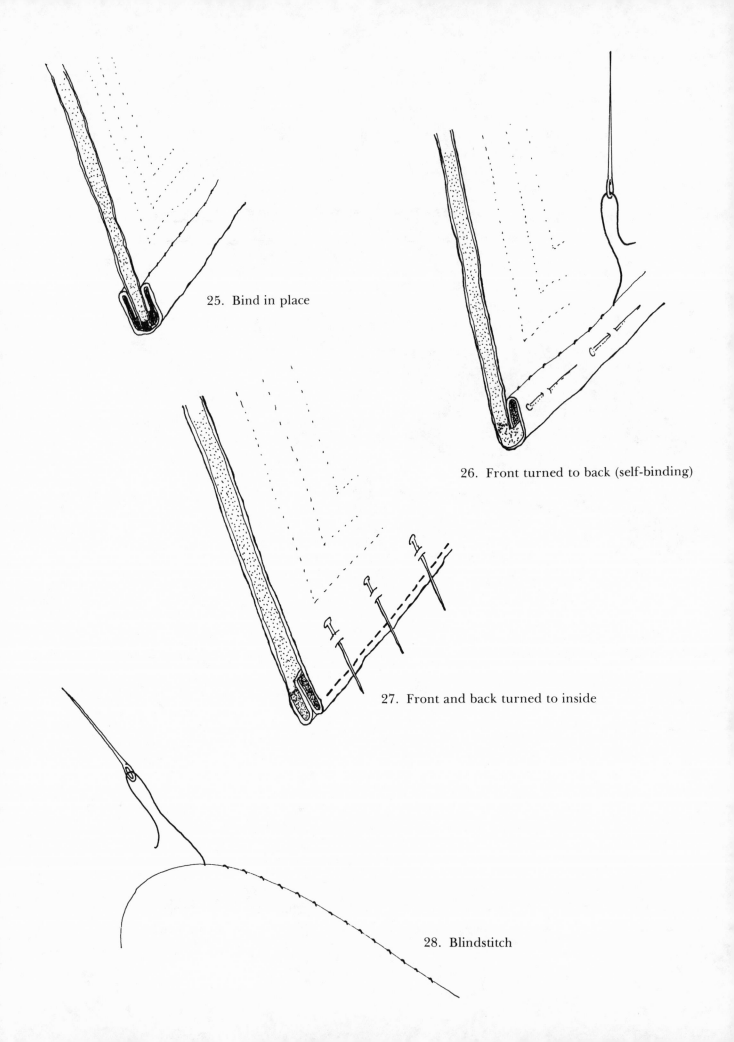

25. Bind in place

26. Front turned to back (self-binding)

27. Front and back turned to inside

28. Blindstitch

FINISHING THE EDGES

In the old days, the edges of the quilt were nearly always finished off with strips of binding because they were often shredded from being stretched so tightly on the frame and they had to be neatly enclosed in new fabric to prevent unraveling. Binding is still my favorite method of finishing, but I'll give you a choice.

BINDING

Cut strips of fabric 1″ to 5″ wide, sufficient to go all around the quilt. The width depends purely on what you think will look best. There's no need to cut on the bias unless the quilt has curved or angled edges. Pin-baste strips of binding, right sides against the quilt top, through all layers, as shown. Sew through all layers, preferably by machine. Be sure that you have pinned the strip at least every 3″; otherwise the binding strip stretches (always a danger with very long lengths of fabric). Sew the long sides first, then the ends. You can miter the corners, or just sew the end pieces straight across the sides.

Turn the binding to the back of the quilt, turn under a narrow hem, and pin-baste carefully all around the quilt. Hand-sew the hem in place using a blind stitch.

SELF-BINDING

If you prefer, you can trim the backing to make it ½″ shorter than the top. Turn the top edge to the back, turn under a narrow hem, and blind-stitch in place.

Or trim the top so that the backing is wider by ½″ all around the quilt. Turn the ½″ of backing over onto the front, roll and baste a ¼″ hem, and secure with a blind stitch.

MACHINE FINISHING

If you like, you can turn a narrow hem on both top and backing to the inside of the quilt, as shown. Pin all around and topstitch in place, using a thread to match the border on the spool and thread to match the backing on the bobbin. Have the top of the quilt up as you sew. Otherwise the bobbin thread will be the one that shows on top, and it is often not so even as the top thread when many layers are sewn and the thread tension is imperfectly adjusted.

CARING FOR THE QUILT

If you have put in enough quilting, the best way to care for a new quilt in good condition is to wash it and dry it by machine. Dry cleaning tends to shorten the life of the fabrics, although you will have to choose that course if your quilt is too large for a washing machine or if you have not used washable fabrics.

If you wash and dry by hand, do the washing in the bath tub and rinse at least five times. Do not squeeze or wring a quilt; that will snap the quilting stitches. Lay it out to dry on a bushy lawn in the sun, or support it *by two or more parallel clotheslines* so the entire weight of the waterlogged quilt is not dragging in one direction.

Never iron a quilt. This tends to crush down the batting, destroying the puffy quilted effect you have worked to achieve. With polyester batting it is a disaster; the batting melts. Ditto for nylon thread.

Between cleanings the best place for a quilt is on a bed or wall. But it is best not to position it so that it is constantly exposed to direct sunlight. Any dye will fade in the sun eventually, but some of your trendy modern chemical dyes look one hundred years old in a year, and I don't know of any way to tell beforehand which ones they are.

If the quilt is to be folded away, it should be wrapped in tissue paper or a sheet, not plastic. Plastic will hold moisture and may cause mildew. Once or twice a year take the quilt out for airing and refold it with the creases in new places. And remember to sign and date the quilt with indelible ink or embroidery thread, because it may last for centuries and the world will want to know who you were.

The Designs

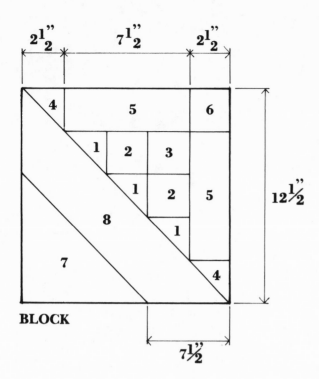

BLOCK

PIECING

1. Sew **1** to **2** to **3**. Press. Sew **1** to **2** to **1**. Press. Sew **1–2–1** to **1–2–3,** basting at the joints.
2. Sew **4** to **5** (2×). Sew **4–5** to **3–2–1**. Sew **6** to **5–4**. Press, and add to **1–2–3–4–5.**
3. Sew **7** to **8**. Press. Sew the diagonal seam to complete the block.

King's Crown

Size: 80″ × 80″ including 5″ border
Sewing: easy
344 pieces: quick

This pattern is made with pieced blocks turned in different directions, alternating with plain blocks. If you prefer, you could have all the pieced blocks going in the same direction, which would cause lovely diagonals to march across the quilt, or you could turn the blocks every which way and create an abstract. If you want to monkey with the pattern, color in the blocks on tracing paper as usual, then cut them apart and start shifting them around.

The name of this block suggests that it may date from the time when America was still part of a kingdom, or it may simply have looked like a crown to whomever made it up. I recommend that you make the block 12½″ square because the block is a five-patch. That means it is easiest to draw if you make it in some multiple of five (12½ = 5 × 2½). I thought 10″ would make the quilt too small, and 15″ would be too big for such a simple block.

In the alternate blocks I chose to set in squares of printed fabric framed by white strips, as shown on p. 71, instead of leaving all-white plain blocks. You could do the same, or you could design a simple piecework pattern to go in the blanks, or you could decorate them with appliqué or with elaborate quilting.

Spinning Jenny

Size: 62″ × 82″ including 2″ and 4″ plain borders
Sewing: medium
428 pieces: quick

A spinning jenny is a machine with many spindles that spins wool or cotton, an industrial version of the spinning wheel. I put the **B** blocks into this design to form unexpected shapes where the two blocks meet, to stop the spinning, and to create an insurrection among the machinery. For some reason spinning jennies remind me of a quatrain about textile mills from the robber-baron era of our history:

> *The golf links lie so near the mill*
> *That almost every day*
> *The laboring children can look out*
> *And see the men at play.*

These are blocks of my own devising. I have recommended that you make them 10″ square; that is large enough to be easy to sew but tight enough to make the motion of the pattern intense, which it is meant to be. If you use 10″ for the scale, the block part of the patchwork will be 50″ × 70″, and you can add borders of any size. If you want to make the block larger, make it 12½″ or 15″ (the number must be easily divided into fifths).

PIECING

Shapes **1** and **2** in block **A** and shape **2** in block **B** must be cut with care to avoid mirror images of the shape you need (see p. 38). Both blocks are made in four quadrants. In block **A**, you should test-baste all seams before you sew until you are sure you are laying them up right (see p. 44).

For each block sew **1** to **2** to **3**. Press. Repeat (3×) and join four quadrants, basting at joints.

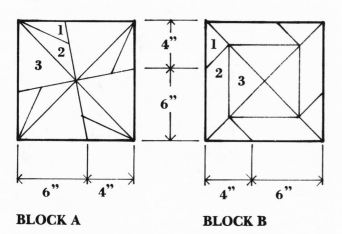

BLOCK A   **BLOCK B**

Cynthia Ann Dancing

Size: 60″ × 80″
Sewing: medium
1,152 pieces

This pattern begins with the traditional *Variable Star* block. In the plate of *Cynthia Ann Dancing,* facing p. 18, you will see that I made my design by putting four conventional blocks in the center of the quilt. As your eye travels out from the center, you find that the blocks remain the same, but the colors begin to drop out. To top, bottom, left, and right of the four center blocks are two blocks each with the blue dropped out and replaced by white. Forming a diamond around those are blocks with both blue and brown dropped out, and finally all around the outside is the same block with only the red shape remaining. When I squint at the quilt, the red shapes look to me like ladies dancing.

In plate I, facing p. 18, you can see the working drawing of another quilt made with the same block and the same technique, *Frank and Nancy's Quilt.* Among other things it differs in having seven blocks by eight, instead of six by eight as there are here. That would seem to have an intolerably large number of pieces in it, but actually, when you design in such a way that two or three adjacent shapes are to be cut from the same material and sewn back together again, you might just as well make a new template and cut them out in one piece. For example, in the outside blocks of *Cynthia Ann Dancing* I was able to cut all the 1–2 shapes as one and all the 4–5–6 shapes as one, so the block at that stage had only twelve pieces in it instead of twenty-four. I didn't put a length of project rating on the design, because I thought you might choose the same technique.

PIECING

Notice that **1** and **3, 4** and **6** are not identical, although they will look very similar. Also notice that **1** and **6, 3** and **4** are mirror images of each other. Review p. 38 and label your templates carefully as you make them. Test-baste all seams until you are sure you have them right (see p. 45).

1. Sew **1** to **2** to **3**. Press. Sew **4** to **5** to **6**. Press.

2. Sew **1-2-3** to **4-5-6**. Press. Clip away some of the excess seam margins where the points of the triangles come together. This will make it easier later to join the long seams.

3. Complete the other three quadrants in the same manner. Sew two quadrants together, basting at the joint. Press. Sew the longer diagonal seam, basting with special care at the center point. Press.

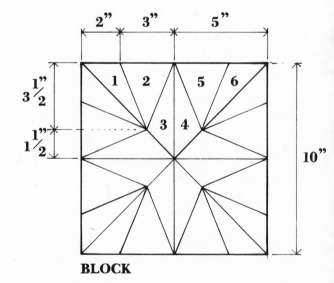

BLOCK

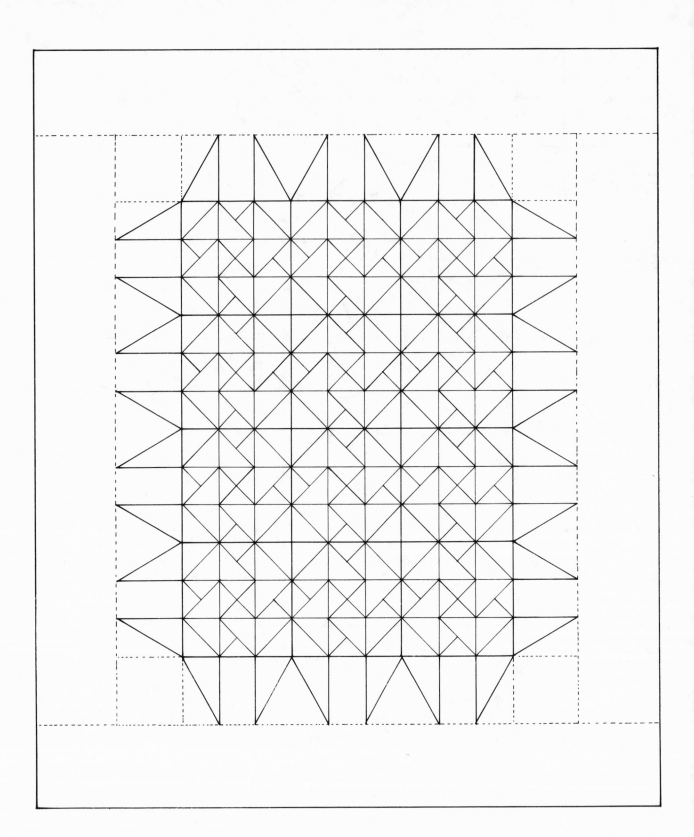

Crow's Nest

Size: 71½" × 86"
Sewing: easy
366 pieces: quick

This quilt is made from an original nine-patch block of Jeffrey's. His first version, called *Card Trick* (facing p. 19), looks like a scrap quilt, but in fact it has a carefully controlled palette of some sixteen colors that repeat from block to block in a regular rhythm. *Card Trick* has no background; instead the colors appear to fan out over the whole surface, overlapping each other like a poker hand.

Crow's Nest is made with exactly the same block (the same line art), but this time Jeffrey chose to use only four colors woven against a white background (facing p. 19). The pointy-toed border is of course different from *Card Trick*'s, but not much. The border grew out of the patchwork, then by looking like crow's feet it gave the quilt its name.

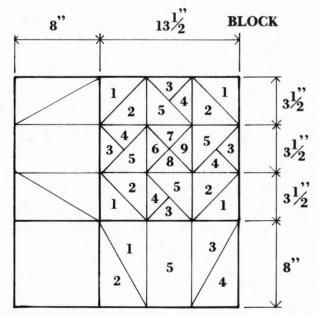

PIECED BORDER

PIECING

1. Sew **1** to **2** (4×). Press.
2. Sew **3** to **4** (4×). Press. Sew **3–4** to **5** (4×). Press.
3. Sew **6** to **7** and **8** to **9**. Press, and join **6–7** to **8–9**, taking care to match the seams.
4. Join the top row of the block, sewing **1–2** to **3–4–5**, then adding **1–2** on the opposite side. Press.
5. Join **3–4–5** to **6–7–8–9**. Add **3–4–5** to the other side.
6. Sew the bottom row as the top (see step 4). Join the three rows, basting carefully at the joints. Press.

PIECING THE BORDER

Remember, when you are piecing long diagonals like the seam between **1** and **2**, that you must experiment a little to be sure you are laying them up right. Test-baste a **1** to a **2**, or a **3** to a **4**, and see if the resulting rectangle matches **5**. It should, so if it doesn't, keep trying (see p. 45).

Piece four border units and join them to the left side of the finished top, basting joints carefully. Repeat for right side. Then piece the top strip, including the blank corner squares, and sew it on, matching joints carefully. Press and repeat for bottom border strip.

Carefully measure and cut the wide border strips. Don't tear; it isn't accurate enough. Pin-baste these thoroughly to the patchwork before you sew them on; if you do not, the plain strips will stretch and you will be sorry.

PIECING

1. Sew **1** to **2** (2×). Sew **3** to **4** (2×). Press. Sew **5** to **6** (2×). Press.
2. Sew **1–2** to **5–6** (2×). Press. Sew **5–6** to **3–4** (2×). Press. Join the two halves of the block and press.

ASSEMBLING THE STRIP

The strip goes together in diagonal units of three, with a *set* triangle sewn into the upper left and lower right sides of the block, as shown in the strip diagram.

ADDING THE BORDER

Sew two strips of 9 triangles each for top and bottom, and two strips of 11 triangles each for the sides. Pin every 3″ and sew all four strips in place. Last, make the four corner pieces from the 8 remaining triangles (shown in dotted lines on the diagram) and sew them in place.

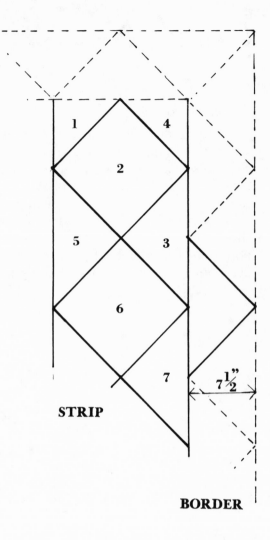

STRIP

BORDER

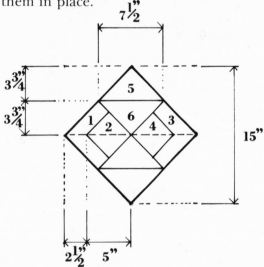

Picket Fence

Size: 90″ × 105″
Sewing: medium
474 pieces: medium

This is a strip quilt, so called because it is assembled in vertical strips. Strip quilts often consist of border strips sewn together to make a piecework design of their own, but this one is a square block turned on the diagonal and set into strips.

Notice, by the way, that when you turn a square up on its end like this, it does not magically become a diamond, although the brightest people you know will call it one. I point this out because lots of people make the mistake when talking about quilts. That doesn't do much harm, but if you make the mistake when cutting and sewing a quilt, using a diamond when you needed a square, you will end up needing expensive psychotherapy. For the record: A square has four equal sides and four right angles. A diamond has four equal sides, but two acute and two obtuse angles. Acute angles are the narrow, pointy ones; obtuse angles are the wide-open ones.

68

East to Eden

Size: 93″ × 108″
Sewing: medium
984 pieces: a major opus

The center panel of this quilt uses a variation of the traditional *Indian Hatchet* block, so I have given the design a name to evoke those halcyon days when the best method men had for killing each other was to hit each other with stone clubs. Block **B** is also traditional; it is usually called *Snowball*. The sewing is actually very easy, except that the outside border block must be laid up carefully, and sometimes those long diagonal seams tend to stretch during sewing. If this happens baste them with pins before sewing. Notice too that **1** and **3** in border **C** are mirror images of each other (see p. 38). There are a lot of pieces in this quilt, it is true, but it's worth the effort. Consider doing the center panel in scraps, surrounded by a fixed color scheme in the two borders to hold it all together.

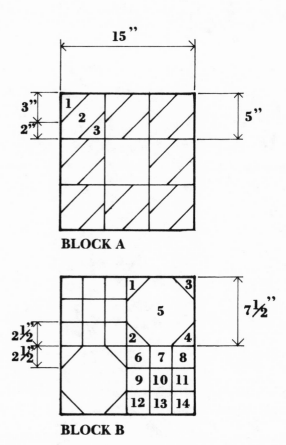

BLOCK A

BLOCK B

PIECING

1. The piecing for **A** is simple. Just sew **1** to **2** to **3** (8×). Press.
2. Join **1–2–3** into three horizontal rows with a blank square in the middle of the middle one. Join the rows, basting at the seams.
3. Piecing **B** is equally simple. The checkerboard quadrant goes together as block **A** does.
4. Sew the four corners onto the octagon, and be sure you are sewing to the corners and not the sides. Press and join the quadrants.

    When all the blocks **A** and **B** are pieced, assemble the central panel of **A** blocks. Then sew the **B** blocks into two strips of four each and two strips of five each. Attach the short strips to the sides of the center panel, basting at each appropriate joint. Press and sew the long strips across top and bottom.

PIECING THE BORDER

1. Test-baste (see p. 45) **1** to **2**. Sew and press (2×). Test-baste and sew **3** to **4** (2×). Press.
2. Sew **1–2** to **3–4** (2×).
3. Lay **1–2–3–4** to **1–2–3–4,** matching the center joint and basting all along the seam. Sew and press.
4. Sew the border units into two strips of five each for the sides and two more of five each with a blank 9″ square at either end for top and bottom. Sew on the side strips first, then the ends, basting at all joints.

I have shown the piece with the corners rounded off, which adds a nice softening echo to the ersatz curves in the *Snowball* block. If you want to do the same, use a string-and-pencil compass. Place the pencil point at the raw edge of seam where the blank square joins the border. Hold the taut string in place at the inside corner of the square, and swing the pencil in an arc to the opposite corner of the block. Trim along the curved pencil line. Use bias tape to bind off (see p. 118).

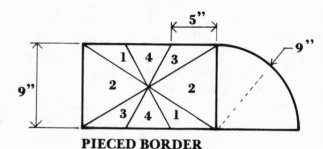

PIECED BORDER

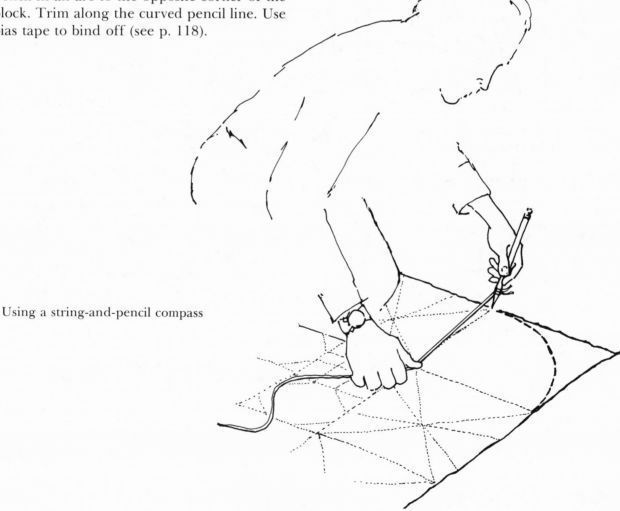

Using a string-and-pencil compass

70

King's Crown, by Beth Gutcheon, 1972 (95″ × 95″)

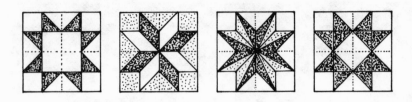

ASSEMBLY DIAGRAM

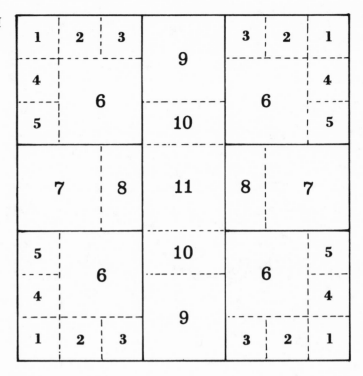

The Star Also Rises

Size: 96″ × 96″
Sewing: easy
558 pieces: medium

The eight-pointed star is one of the commonest figures in American patchwork; trying to find something new to do with it is like trying to find a new harmony for "You Are My Sunshine." This design is my contribution to the literature. The small stars are made with trapezoids while the larger ones are made with the usual squares and triangles, a modest and obvious statement to the effect that there are several ways to skin a cat. Along the border of the page are more variations that you could use in addition or instead.

You will see in the color plate, facing p. 146, that I made this a scrap quilt, meaning that instead of using a few repeating colors I used different combinations for each star. Scrap quilts are fun, but they take longer to make because you have to make as many aesthetic decisions as there are fabrics in the quilt instead of choosing a single color scheme once and for all. Nor can you cut in quantity if you are cutting from dozens of odd-shaped scraps.

Notice that the three stars in the middle are in red and blue, but the shades go from pale to medium to intense. That was supposed to give the illusion of the star exploding outward—I don't know if it works or not. I like it, though.

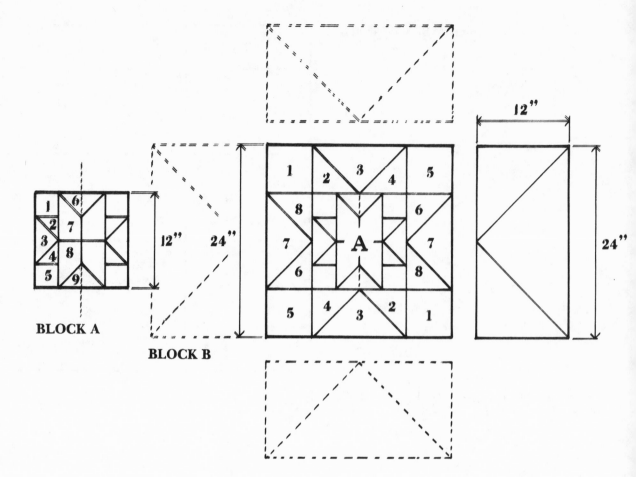

BLOCK A

BLOCK B

PIECING

Start by assembling all of the small stars (block **A**) in vertical strips. Notice that **7** and **8** are mirror images (see p. 38).

1. Sew **1** to **2** to **3** to **4** to **5**. Press.
2. Sew **6** to **7**. Sew **8** to **9**. Press. Join **6–7** to **8–9**. Press.
3. Sew these two strips together, basting at middle joint. Repeat for other half of block. Join middle seam.

ASSEMBLING **B** BLOCKS

1. Sew **1** to **2** to **3** to **4** to **5** (2×). Press.
2. Sew **6** to **7** to **8** (2×). Press.
3. Sew **6–7–8** to a side of a block **A**. Repeat on opposite side.
4. Apply strip **1–2–3–4–5** across top and bottom, basting at joints. Press.

ASSEMBLING FINISHED BLOCKS

In the diagram of the assembly order, p. 73, you can see that the quilt top has four identical corner areas. These are separated by four strips, each consisting of a **B** block and two of the points of the largest star. The points are right-angle triangles measuring 12″ on a side. The background between these large points is a right-angle triangle whose hypotenuse is 24″. You can cut this all in one piece or make it from two 12″ triangles sewn back to back. The center square is a **B** block. Sew the four corner areas by sewing **1–2–3** to **4–5–6**. Sew **7** to **8** (2×) and **9** to **10** (2×). Finish the top in three vertical strips. Sew a corner area to a **7–8**. Add the bottom corner area. Sew **9** to **10** to **11** to **10** to **9**. Press. Sew remaining corners to remaining **7–8**. Press. Join the three strips, basting thoroughly at all joints and in between. Press.

Construction by Molly Upton, 1975 (80″ × 74″)

76

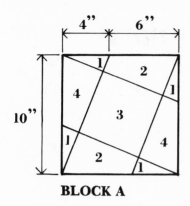

BLOCK A

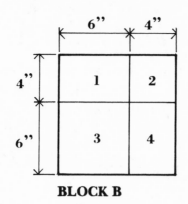

BLOCK B

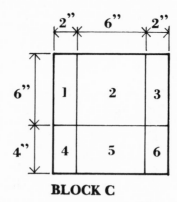

BLOCK C

PIECING

1. For **A**, sew **1** to **2** to **3** (2×). Press. Sew **4** to **3** to **4**. Press.
2. Sew **1-2-1** to **4-3-4** to **1-2-1**.
3. For **B**, sew **1** to **2** and **3** to **4**. Sew **1-2** to **3-4**, basting at the joint.
4. For **C**, sew **1** to **2** to **3**. Press. Sew **4** to **5** to **6**. Press. Sew **1-2-3** to **4-5-6**, basting at joints. Press.

Checkerboard Skew

Size: 60″ × 80″ including 2″ and 3″ plain borders
Sewing: easy
252 pieces: quick

The **A** block in this quilt, the skewed checkerboard, is sometimes known as *Washington's Puzzle.* I've never been sure who was puzzled, the general or the city. My intention in this design was to juxtapose the skewed checkerboards with others seen head on: The latter are on a larger scale than the skew blocks, so you can only see a portion of each block as if there were two planes, with the straight checkerboards partially glimpsed behind the screen of skew blocks.

I have arranged the **B** and **C** blocks in the hope of creating a varied but balanced surface. Feel free to rearrange them; sew all the blocks and then lay them out on the floor and see if there's a way to put them together that you like better than this.

When you cut the pieces for block **A,** remember to get the template the right way up so you won't get mirror images instead of the shape you want (see p. 38). If you do the quilt in the dimensions shown, it will go well on a single bed or on a wall, which is where the original is.

Judy in Arabia

Size: 60″ × 72″ plus whatever you choose to add
by way of borders and binding
Sewing: medium
720 pieces: a substantial undertaking

This is an original design of Jeffrey's. He likes to make patterns that turn up a whole assortment of standard patchwork motifs. This one includes an eight-pointed star, a four-pointed star, a checkerboard, a traditional four-patch block called *Broken Dishes* (where the corners of the real block come together), and big circles that are really made with straight lines. It is named for an exotic and beautiful friend of ours who had just come back from a business trip to the Middle East and saw in it mosques and minarets.

In plate IV, facing p. 19, you can see the finished version as Jeffrey colored it, and in plate I, facing p. 18, you can see his working drawing. The block is a nine-patch. The design is five blocks across and five down, with a half row of blocks at top and bottom. It is arranged this way so that the center of the quilt is the center of a block, rather than a seam between two blocks as it would have been if the design was simply arranged five blocks across and six down.

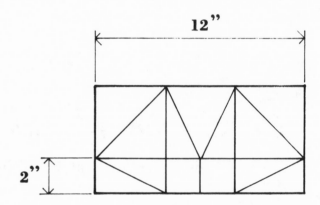

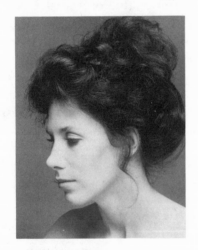

Judy in New York

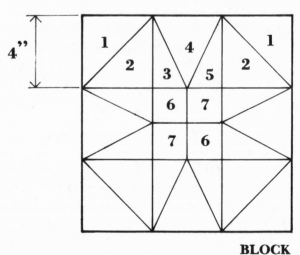

BLOCK

PIECING

1. Sew **1** to **2** (4×). Press.
2. Carefully test-baste **3** to **4** (see p. 45). Sew. Press. Test-baste and sew **4** to **5**. Press and repeat (3×).
3. Sew **6** to **7** (2×). Press. Sew **6–7** to **6–7**. Press.
4. Sew **1–2** to **3–4–5** to **1–2** (2×) to form top and bottom rows.
5. Sew **3–4–5** to **6–7–6–7** to **3–4–5**. Press and sew the three rows together, basting at all joints.

78

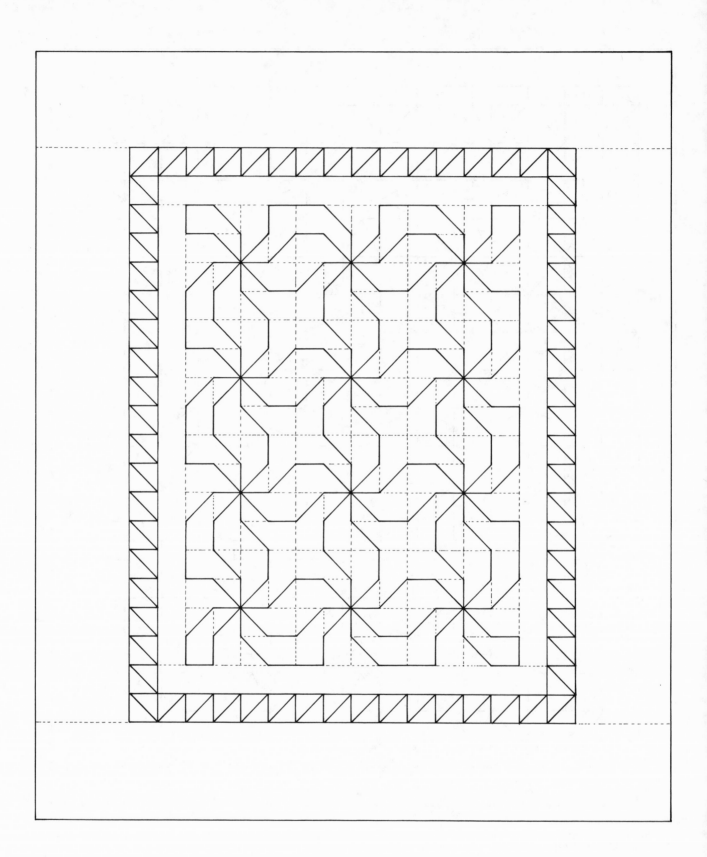

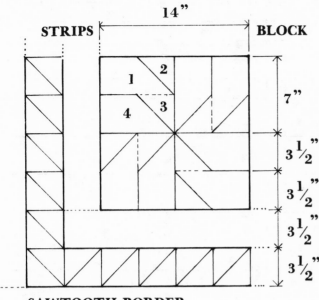

STRIPS **BLOCK**

14"

7"

3½"

3½"

3½"

3½"

SAWTOOTH BORDER

PIECING

Remember to cut trapezoids **2** and **4** with the template the right way up to avoid mirror images (see p. 38).

1. Sew **1** to **2**. Press. Sew **3** to **4**. Press.
2. Sew **1–2** to **3–4**. Press.
3. Repeat for other four quadrants. Sew them together as indicated in diagram. Remember to baste at center joint.

Measure and cut the 3½"-wide plain border strips. Baste the side strips first with a pin every 3". Sew, press, then apply top and bottom strips.

To piece the sawtooth borders, just sew the triangles to each other to make squares, then sew the squares into strips. Count carefully. Baste in place, sides first with many pins; sew, press, then add ends.

Katherine Wheels

Size: 78" × 92" including 11" plain border
Sewing: easy
336 pieces: quick

This is actually a version of the old *Clay's Choice* block (see p. 131). It was named after Henry Clay, but the pattern lasted much longer than Clay did and reappeared in other places and times, called things like *Henry's Star* and then *Star of the West.* Plate XV, facing p. 147, shows this one, which is named after my goddaughter.

This is a simplified version of a medallion quilt, the most popular style of the eighteenth century. Medallion quilts have a center panel surrounded by several different kinds of border strips. If you use the dimensions worked out here, the sawtooth border just rims the top of a double bed, while the plain outside border provides a 12" drop on each side.

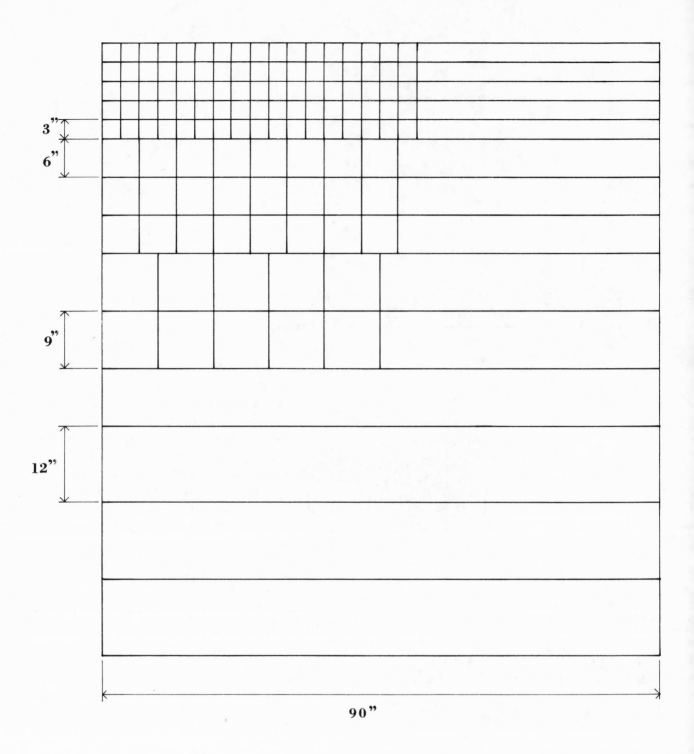

Eight-Pointed Stars, and Stripes by Jeffrey Gutcheon, 1974 (95″ × 105″)
Also shown: Cynthia Ann, (5′ 5″)

America, america

Size: 90″ × 96″
Sewing: easy
133 pieces: quick

Since flags are patchwork anyway, I thought I'd like to make a patchwork Flag. Aside from its stirring philosophical implications, I like this quilt because it makes a bed look eight feet long.

The quilt is assembled in strips. You can make the stripes of the pattern out of a solid piece of fabric, or you could piece one together out of, say, different shades of red or white. If you decide to make the stripes all in one piece, be sure to measure and cut carefully; tearing is not accurate enough for patchwork. And when you are ready to sew the horizontal strips together, be sure to pin-baste at least every 3″ to keep the work from stretching as you sew.

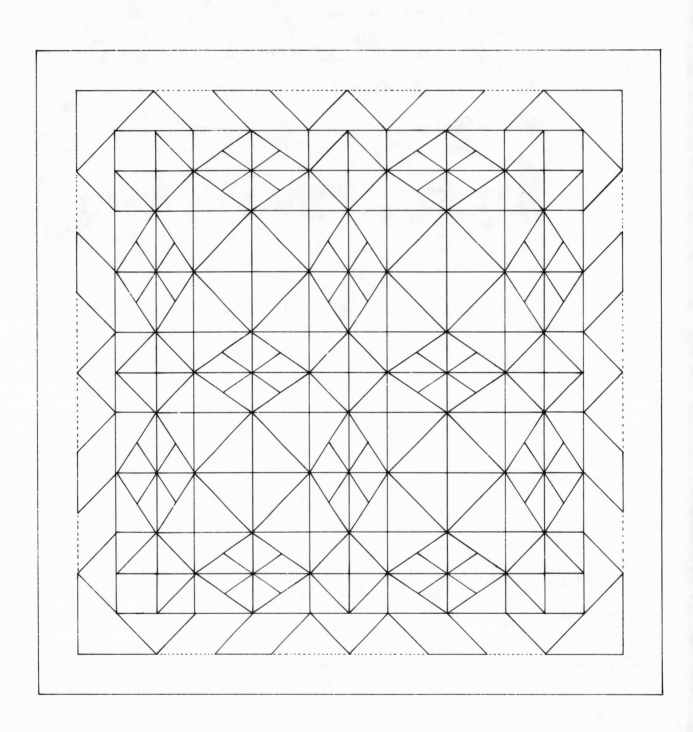

84

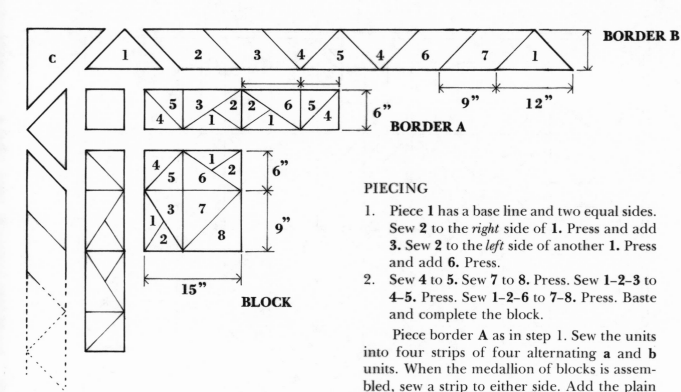

Spiritus Mundi

Size: 96″ × 96″ including 6″ plain border
Sewing: medium
288 pieces: quick

PIECING

1. Piece **1** has a base line and two equal sides. Sew **2** to the *right* side of **1**. Press and add **3**. Sew **2** to the *left* side of another **1**. Press and add **6**. Press.
2. Sew **4** to **5**. Sew **7** to **8**. Press. Sew **1–2–3** to **4–5**. Press. Sew **1–2–6** to **7–8**. Press. Baste and complete the block.

Piece border **A** as in step 1. Sew the units into four strips of four alternating **a** and **b** units. When the medallion of blocks is assembled, sew a strip to either side. Add the plain square to the remaining strips and apply them top and bottom. Remember to baste at the joints. Press.

Assemble border **B** in four identical strips beginning and ending with **1**. Sew a strip to each side of the patchwork, then add the four corner triangles (**c**). Measure and cut the outside border, pin it carefully at least every 3″, then sew it in place.

This pattern is simple in concept but a little tricky to describe. Nevertheless I am going to try to describe it, just in case you don't find the line art crystal clear, to coin a phrase. It's one of Jeffrey's designs, and I found it a little mystifying myself.

The center panel is made of sixteen identical blocks, surrounded by a row of border **A,** and outside that, of border **B**. The blocks rotate so that in the top row, beginning at the left, piece **4** is in the top left corner of the block. In the next block in the row, **4** is in the top right corner. Then back to the top left, then again top right.

The second row is identical to the first but upside down. In the first block **4** is in the bottom left; in the second, bottom right; and so on. Outside this central medallion, border row **A** is made of units from the main block plus a blank square at each corner, and outside that border **B** is composed in four strips beginning and ending with triangle **1**.

When drawing the block to size to make the templates, notice that the line between **1** and **2** goes from the corner to the exact middle of the rectangle. Draw it by placing a straightedge from lower left corner to upper right corner, then draw the line as if you were going to bisect the rectangle. Notice also that **3** and **6** in the block and in border **A** are mirror images, and in border **B**, **2** and **3** are the mirrors of **6** and **7**. Keep this in mind when cutting (see p. 38).

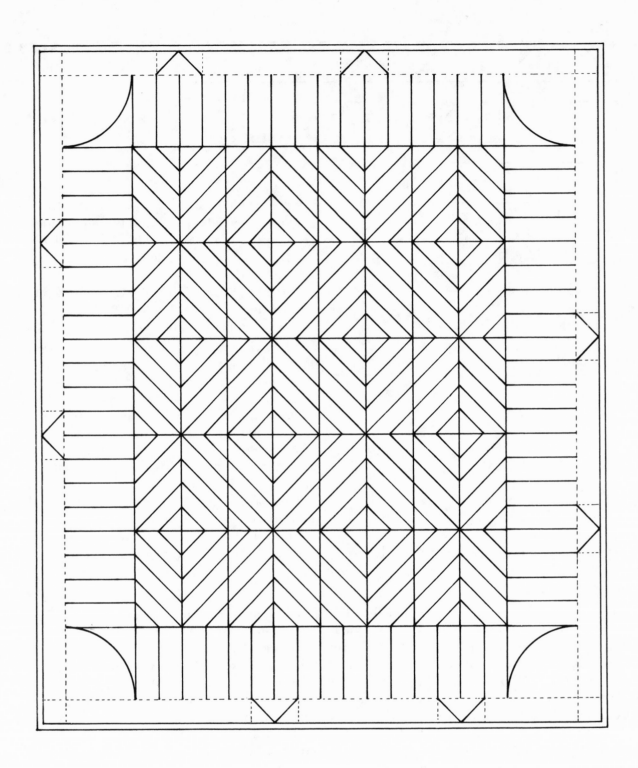

86

Refractions

Size: 72" × 84"
Sewing: not easy
356 pieces: short

This pattern is, as they say, deceptively simple. In plate IX, facing p. 146, you will see how Jeffrey colored in the blocks. You will notice also that the patchwork isn't quite finished. We often make the medallion of a quilt and tack it on the wall so we can live with it for a while before making a decision about borders and quilting patterns. In this case, that mysterious internal process has so far lasted two and a half years. As you can see from the drawing, he has now completed the border design, and I have every confidence that he will hit on a quilting pattern at least by the summer of 1978.

Here is why the sewing is tricky, even though it looks simple. If you cut the pieces on the bias, their sides stretch, which makes piecing difficult. If you cut them straight with the weave, the slanted ends will be on the bias and *they* will stretch, making it hard to match up the seams at the joints. This problem can be solved with old-fashioned thread-basting, which never killed anybody, and especially since there are not that many pieces in the quilt, you will have plenty of time to be a little more rigorous than usual in your sewing methods if it seems necessary.

It also happens that laying up the blocks is harder than it looks. Look at the first block in the upper left corner. When you lay its two rectangular halves right sides together to sew the vertical seam, their slanting seams correspond and are easily matched. Now look at the seam between block **1** and block **2.** When you lay those two blocks right sides together, the seams all crisscross because the lines of **1** are heading up from lower left to upper right while the lines of **2** turned right side down, will run from upper left down to the right. This means that to get the joints to look perfect, you have to pin each one so that the seams cross ¼" from the raw edge, where the new seam will fall.

Having said all that, let me emphasize what I said in the general instructions; none of this work is *very* difficult. By very difficult, I mean something you can't do right no matter how hard you try. You can do this perfectly well if you are scrupulous about cutting and basting.

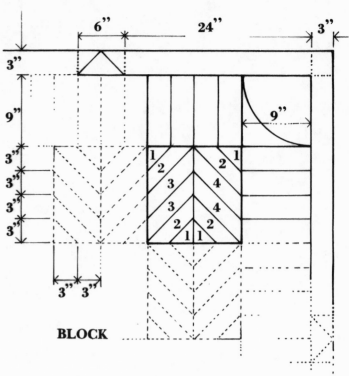

OUTER BORDER

BLOCK

FIRST BORDER

PIECING

In cutting, be aware that **3** and **4** are mirrors of each other (review p. 38).

1. Sew **1** to **2** (2×). Press.
2. Test-baste **2** to **3** (see p. 45). Sew and press (2×).
3. Test-baste and sew **1–2–3** to **1–2–3**. Press.
4. Repeat for mirror side of the block, substituting **4** for **3**. Sew vertical seam between the two, basting at joints.

THE INNER BORDER

The first border consists of 9″ × 3″ oblong strips and corner blocks with arcs. For each of these blocks cut one 9½″ square in the color you want for the background, shape **a,** and a second 9½″ square in the color you want for the fan-shaped piece **b.** Using a string-and-pencil compass (see p. 70), swing an arc from corner to corner of the square you cut for shape **b** and cut the drawn curve. Pin **b** to **a** with straight edges matching, turn under ¼″ hem on the curved edge of **b,** and sew it in place by hand with an invisible hemming stitch.

THE OUTER BORDER

The outside border is a 3″-wide strip interrupted by triangle shapes that echo and complete triangle shapes in the medallion. Measure the patchwork to find the length of the strips between the triangles; then measure and cut them carefully (do not tear). Pin thoroughly before you sew these borders onto the quilt top; long strips such as these tend to stretch if they are not well basted.

Road to Paradise, by Rose Dwight, 1976 (45″ × 72″) (Now look at *Judy in Arabia* facing page 19.)

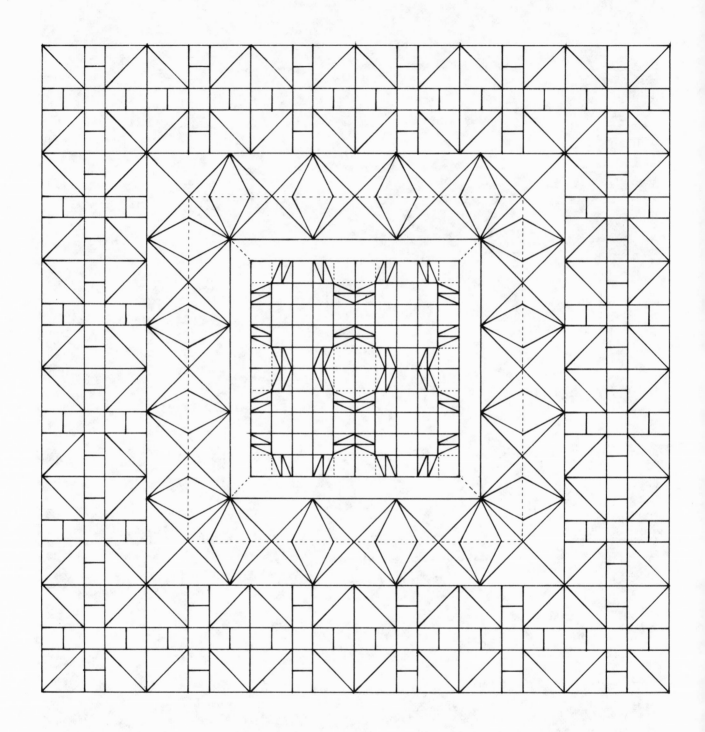

Pigeon Toes Medallion

Size: 90″ × 90″
Sewing: not easy
692 pieces: medium

This design is special to me for several reasons. First, the figure at the very center, where all the pigeon toes come together, looks very much like a symbol from Tantric art representing feminine wisdom. Second, I first made the *Pigeon Toes* pattern on the occasion of the wedding of two old and very dear friends (they were marrying each other). There are few things in life more satisfying than having people you love, love each other. It hardly ever happens, though. Just think, if all your friends married each other, you'd only have to send out half as many Christmas cards.

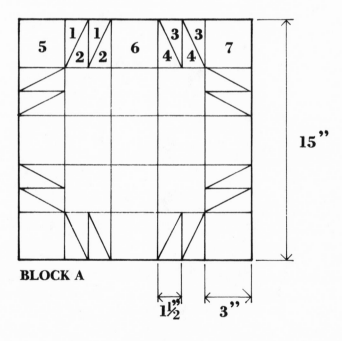

BLOCK A

PIECING

The *Pigeon Toes* block is tricky because each pair of toes must be test-basted (see p. 45) in such a way that the rectangle they form is exactly 3″ long. Somehow it's hard to get them right because they're so small. You have to keep your mind on it.

BLOCK A

1. Test-baste **1** to **2,** and sew and press (8×). Join **1–2** to **1–2** (4×).
2. Test-baste and sew **3** to **4** (8×). Press. Sew **3–4** to **3–4** (4×). Press.
3. Sew the top row of the block: **5** to **1–2–1–2** to **6** to **3–4–3–4** to **7**. Press.
4. Complete the rest of the rows one at a time, following the diagram. Join the rows, basting carefully at each joint.

Join the four **A** blocks that form the inner medallion.

Carefully measure and cut four plain strips 3½″ wide and 36½″ long. Center and pin these along the sides of the medallion, with a pin every 3″. I have departed here from my usual practice of going to any lengths to avoid sewing around angles, because the design seemed to demand diagonals here and in the adjacent border row. That makes a total of eight angles to sew—just enough to be interesting. (It's really only hard when you have to do it ninety times.)

Sew the strips in place; begin and end each seam ¼″ from the raw edge of the

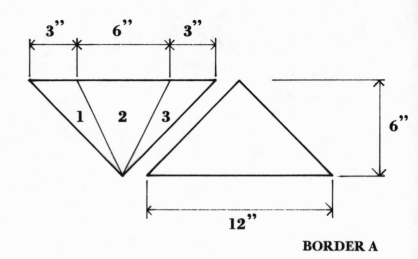

BORDER A

medallion. Knot or backstitch to lock each seam at beginning and end. Miter the corners (see p. 53), pin them, then sew the diagonal by machine, or by hand with an invisible hemming stitch.

PIECE BORDER A IN TWO STRIPS

1. Be sure to test-baste every seam in this border until you are sure you have the hang of it. Sew **1** to **2**. Add **3** and press. You need 32 **1–2–3** units in all.

2. I have labeled the **1–2–3** unit **a** and the matching plain triangle **b.** Sew four strips **a,b,a,b,a,b,a.** Remember to test-baste, and pin the edge if you have trouble with stretching.

3. Center these four strips at the sides of the medallion, baste thoroughly, and sew. Begin and end ¼″ from the edge and lock the seams fore and aft. Press. Baste and sew the diagonal corner seams. Be careful that the seams at the corners butt right up to each other, but do not let them cross, as that causes a pucker, and do not leave too great a gap between them, because that causes a hole.

4. Sew four more strips **a,b,a,b,a,b,a.** Center and sew them in place. Sew two **b** triangles side by side to make a larger triangle (4×). These will form the outside corners of the **A** border, as you see on the line drawing. Sew these four large **bb** triangles in place.

PIECING BORDER B

1. Sew **1** to **2** (4×). Sew **3** to **4** (4×). Press.
2. Sew **1–2** to **3–4,** and add **1–2** to form the top row of the block. Press.
3. For the middle row sew **3–4** to **5** to **3–4.** Press. Make the bottom row the same as the top. Join the three rows.

    Sew two strips of four blocks each. Add them to the sides of the quilt. Sew the remaining strips of six blocks each. Add them to top and bottom.

    I know that looks like a lot to go through, but it's more fun than it sounds.

BORDER B

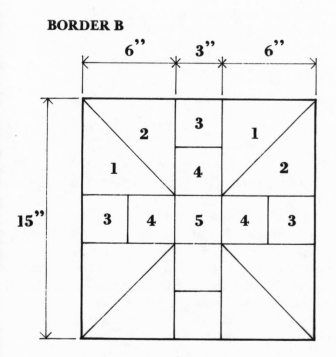

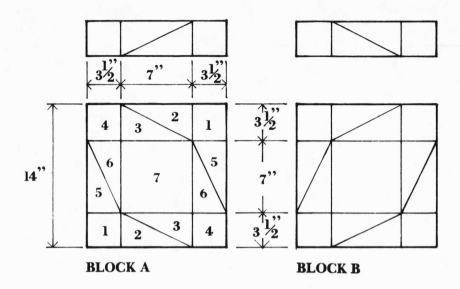

BLOCK A   **BLOCK B**

PIECING

This block goes together in strips.

1. Sew **2** to **3** (2×). Press. Then add **1** and **4** at either end (2×).
2. Sew **5** to **6** (2×). Press. Sew **5–6** onto either side of **7**.
3. Sew **1–2–3–4** to top and bottom of **5–6–7–6–5,** basted at joints. Press.

Dragonfly

Size: 70″ × 90″ plus borders
Sewing: medium
430 pieces: medium

This is an original design by Jeffrey; at first we called it *Wagon Wheels* because the first version he made looked like big wheels with sheriff's stars. It's very versatile, and we've made three versions of it already.

It has five rows across and six rows down, with a border row at top and bottom consisting of a repeat of the top strip of the blocks. Block **B** is the same as block **A** turned through 90°. In our version block **A** has one repeating color scheme, and block **B** another. You use the same cutting templates for each, but remember to pay attention to which side of the template is up when you are cutting; pieces **5** and **6** are mirror images of **2** and **3**.

The sewing is not really hard at all, but you have to take some care about laying up the long triangles. Test-baste **2** to **3** (see pp. 44, 45) to be sure the resulting rectangle matches square **7,** to which it will presently be sewn. If it doesn't, remove the pins and adjust the triangles until they come out right. Sew the seam, then use that piece as a model for basting the others.

95

96

Flying Dutchman

Size: 60″ × 72″ including 2″ and 4″ plain borders
Sewing: easy
552 pieces: medium

This is a traditional block named after the legend of the Dutch mariner who was condemned to sail the seas until the Day of Judgment. His ghost ship, *The Flying Dutchman,* was sometimes sighted at sea, and it was considered a very bad omen. I had a friend who was writing a novel about life (or whatever it was) aboard *The Flying Dutchman.* Someone had lent him a house at the shore, and he was going to live the penultimate literary life, making great art all day, then rewarding himself at night with a stroll to the corner pub and a few carefree hours with his colorful fishermen neighbors. At the end of four months he had fixed a lot of broken shutters, made a lot of phone calls, drunk a lot of beer, and written about thirty pages. And the moral of that story is: It is not the absence of the perfect life-style that prevents us from making our art; it's us.

PIECING

1. Sew **1** to **2,** then **3** to **4.** Press. Sew **1–2** to **3–4,** basting at the joint. Press.
2. Sew **5** to **6** to **7.** Press. Sew **5–6–7** to **4.** Press.
3. Sew **8** to **1–2–3–4–5–6–7.** Press. Repeat for other three quadrants.

Follow the piecing chart to make the border strips. Sew **1** to **2,** and press. Sew **3** to **4** to **5.** Press, and sew **1–2** to **3–4–5,** basting at the joint. And so on.

Follow the line carefully in making the pieced border corners. Add the side strips of four border units each first, then add the top and bottom strips, consisting of three border units plus corners. Baste carefully at each joint. Press, carefully baste, and sew the plain strips.

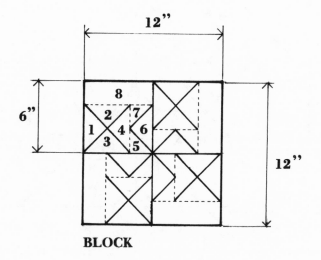

BLOCK

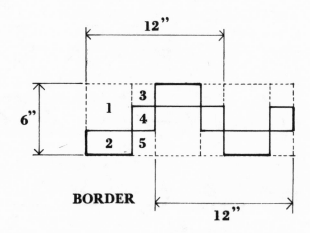

BORDER

Neighbors

Size: 78" × 90"
Sewing: easy
760 pieces: substantial

This quilt is based on an old block called *Next Door Neighbor*. The dotted lines are construction lines (seam lines) added by me to make the block go together with straight seams. You can see that this amounts to four extra pieces per block to cut and sew. The advantages are that the sewing is far easier (even if there is more of it) than if you sew the block the traditional way and that the extra seam adds an extra geometric shape, which you can color in such a way as to alter the design. But I have also given you the block the traditional way, with the pieces numbered in order for piecing. If you want to try setting in angles, just ignore the dotted lines when you color the line art and follow the traditional piecing instructions.

PIECING

Beware of cutting the mirror image of piece **1** in the block (see p. 38). Sew **1** to **2**. Press. Sew **3** to **4** to **5**. Press. Sew **1–2** to **3–4–5**. Repeat for other three quadrants.

PIECING THE BORDERS

First sew triangles onto the ends of the rectangles, as the drawing shows, then join these three-part units into long strips. Make the strips for the sides first. You will notice that at the bottom left and top right end of the side strips one of the rectangles is truncated (see where the dotted lines are in the line art). Don't bother to make a special cutting for those; just make regular rectangles and sew across them with the top and bottom strips of border. Then cut off the extra part of the piece underneath the work.

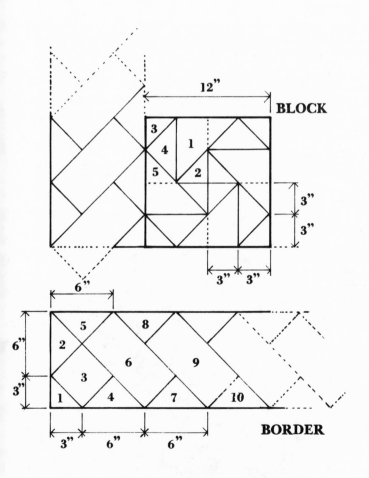

99

TRADITIONAL BLOCK

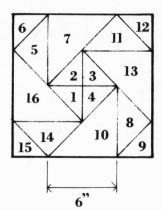

6"

TRADITIONAL PIECING

1. Sew **1** to **2.** Sew **3** to **4.** Press. Join **1–2** and **3–4.** Press.
2. Sew **5** to **6** to **7.** Sew **8** to **9** to **10.** Sew **11** to **12** to **13.** Sew **14** to **15** to **16.** Press.
3. Sew **5–6–7** to **2** and press.
4. Sew **8–9–10** to **4;** press.
5. Sew **11–12–13** into its place as follows: first join **11** to **7,** stopping exactly at the corner of the seam (do not sew out to the raw edge). Leave the needle in the down position, piercing the seam at the corner. Rotate the work so that you can match the edges of **13** and **3.** Sew the seam. Press. Repeat for **14–15–16.** Press.

Down along the rural route
Everybody's talkin'
Henry Jones has been thrown out
They say this time he's walkin'
I don't know about Henry Jones
But it sounds like a rumor to me
Talk is cheap
But that don't mean it's free.
R. O. Curtis

Vivid Coastline, by Susan Hoffman, 1974 (78″ × 75″)

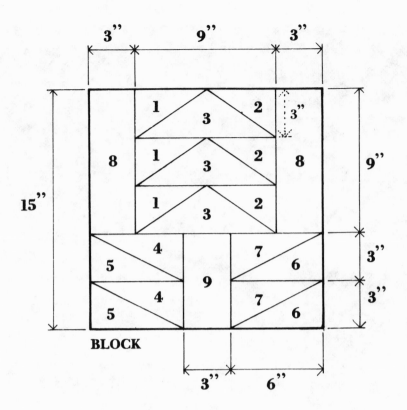

BLOCK

PIECING

1. Sew **1** to **2** to **3** (3×). Press. Sew **1–2–3** to **1–2–3** to **1–2–3.** Add **8** on either side and press.

2. Sew **4** to **5** (2×). Sew **6** to **7** (2×). Press. Sew **4–5** to **4–5.** Sew **6–7** to **6–7.** Press. Join these units to either side of **9.** Press.

3. Lay up the two sections. Try to center **9** in the middle of **3** as well as you can by eye. (This is more important than having the edges match.) Baste, sew, and press.

The Forest for the Trees

Size: 84″ × 99″
Sewing: easy
448 pieces: medium

This pattern is based on a traditional *Pine Tree* block. The plain inner border is 3″ wide, and the outer border is 9″ wide. It's easy to sew. Just remember in cutting that shapes **4** and **5** are mirror images of **7** and **6** (see p. 38). And when you lay up those long triangles, do a test to make sure the finished rectangle will be 6″ long (see p. 45 for test-basting).

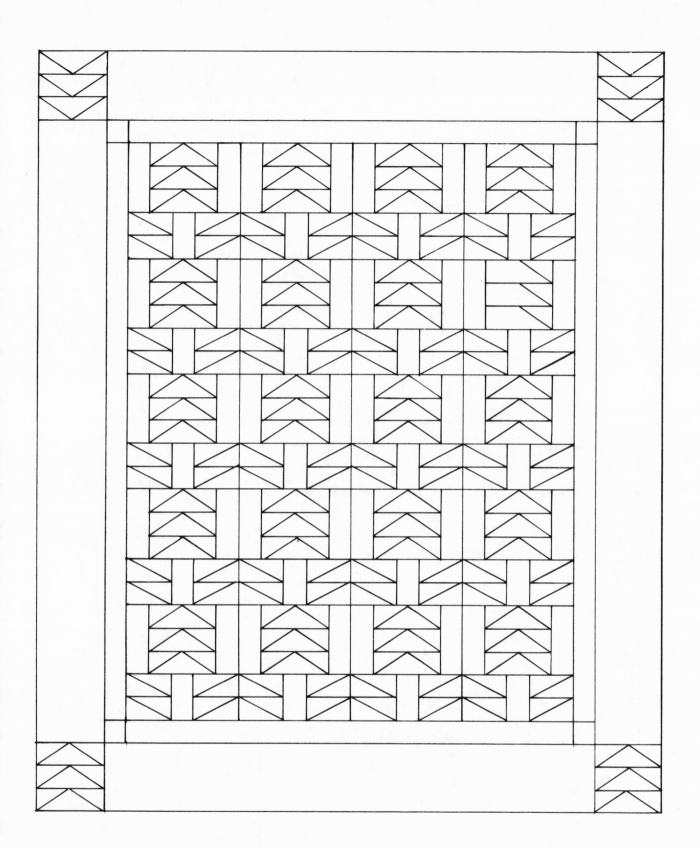

103

PIECING

As the chart shows, you first construct the central square within the block, then the corners. Add the upper right and lower left corners first, then the remaining ones.

1. Test-baste (see p. 45), then sew **1** to **2** (2×). Press. Test-baste and sew **3** to **4** (2×). Press. Sew **1–2–3–4** to **1–2–3–4,** basting carefully at the center joint. Press.
2. Sew **5** to **6** (2×). Sew **5** to **8** (2×). Press. Test-baste and sew **5–6** to **7** to **5–8** (2×). Press.
3. Sew **9** to **10** (4×). Press. Sew **9–10** to **11** (2×). Sew **9–10** to **13** (2×). Then test-baste and sew these units to **12** (2×).
4. Sew **5–6–7–8–5** to upper right corner of central square, basting at joints. Repeat for opposite corner. Press.
5. Add **9–10–11–12–13–10–9** to remaining sides. Press.

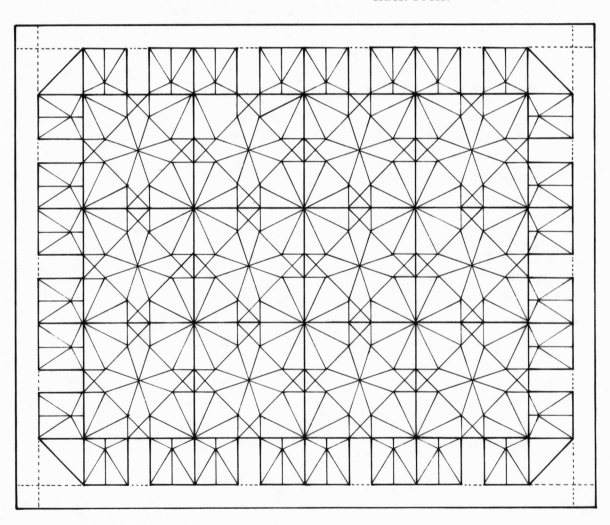

104

Assemble the border units in groups, as shown in the diagram. Best test-baste **1** to **2** and **4** to **5** until you are sure you have the lay-up right. When all border units are finished, assemble two strips of four units each, and sew them to the sides of the patchwork, basting at each joint. Sew two remaining strips of three border units plus corner squares, and join them to top and bottom, basting carefully. Press.

Measure and cut and piece two border strips 4½" wide and 76½" long and two 4½" wide and 96½" long. (Actually, you had better measure your patchwork before you make these strips since the finished dimensions may vary from the projected ones.) Sew the long strips to the sides of the quilt, pinning every 3" to prevent stretching. Sew the shorter strips, plus corner squares, across top and bottom.

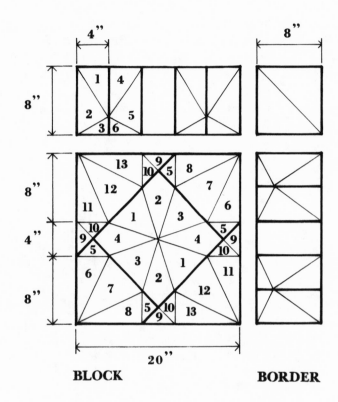

BLOCK   BORDER

Here Is the Steeple

Size: 84" × 104" including 4" border
Sewing: fairly difficult
578 pieces: medium

Cole Porter used to be hauled into court by indignant songwriters who would hammer out some awful ballad with two bars the same as two bars from "Night and Day," then demand that the court convict Porter of plagiarism. He got so tired of it that eventually he claimed to have given up listening to anyone's music but his own, being the only way to prove he couldn't have stolen so much as a phrase. Patchwork is sort of like music in that it is all composed of a surprisingly small number of basic elements that can be arranged and rearranged in a surprisingly vast number of ways. I actually believe that I have invented this block, but after three hundred years and several million American quilts, it seems unlikely that there's anything left to invent. So it's probably a melody I picked up somewhere. ("Only yooo beneath the moooon La-la-la-laaa"—Move over, Cole.)

In order to draw this block to size for making templates, you will most likely have to tape several pieces of graph paper together (see p. 31). Notice that **6** and **8** in the block are mirror images, as are **11** and **13**; so are **1** and **4**, **2** and **5**, and **3** and **6** in the border. Review p. 38 and cut carefully.

Lightning

Size: 78″ × 92″ including 8″ and 10″ plain borders
Sewing: easy
328 pieces: quick

There's a famous old pattern called *Drunkard's Path* because it cuts a wobbly swath across the quilt top. It was almost always done in white and Turkey red. Turkey red dye was bright and fast and named for the country, but I always associate it with the bird, anyway. I've always admired *Drunkard's Path,* but didn't care to sew so many curved seams, so I made this pattern from it by straightening out the curves. The sewing is a snap and it goes very fast, so this is a good beginner's project. Also, it looks fine in practically any kind of room. You may prefer to make more blocks and keep narrower borders. Or you can change the size of the block, though I wouldn't make them smaller than 6″ or larger than 8″.

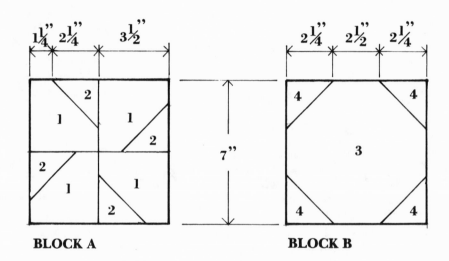

BLOCK A   **BLOCK B**

PIECING

1. In block **A,** sew **1** to **2** (4×). Join quadrants.
2. In block **B,** sew corner pieces **4** onto **3,** (4×). Pay attention that you are really sewing them onto the corners and not onto the sides. They look almost the same, but in fact the sides are slightly longer. Check them against your template if you're confused.

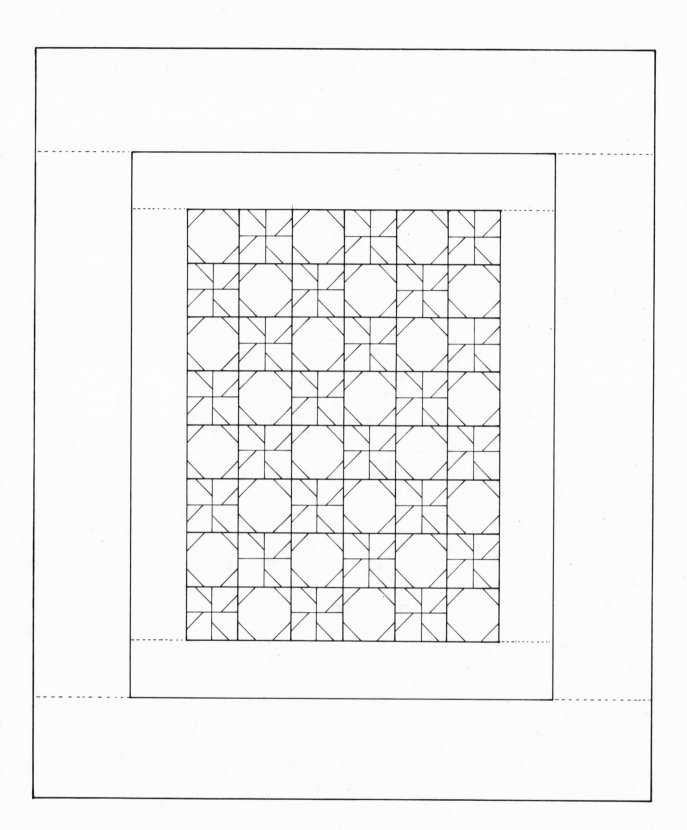

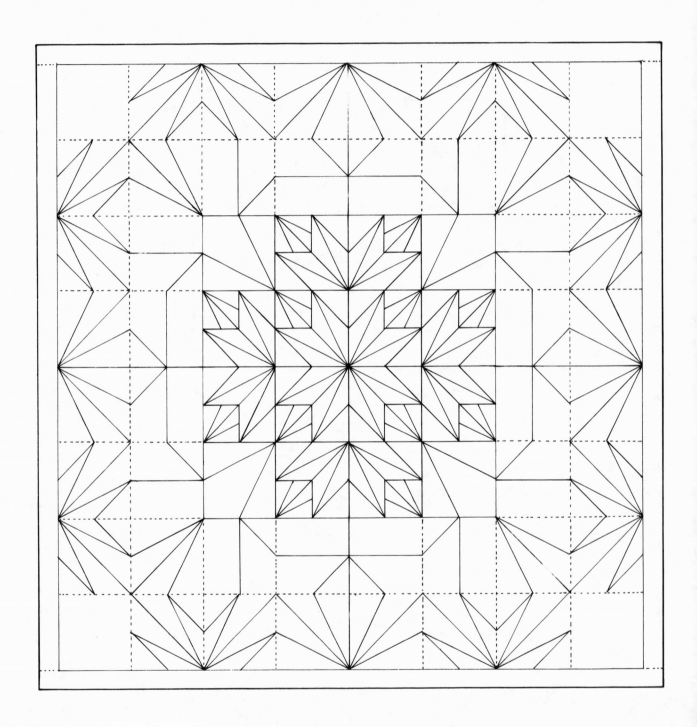

108

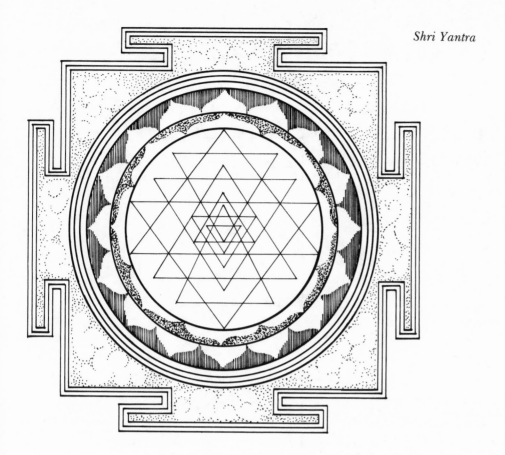

Yantra

Size: 96″ × 96″ plus binding
Sewing: not easy
324 pieces: quick

A mantra is a special word or prayer sound that you make over and over in your brain while meditating. It helps turn off the chatter in your mind and opens the way for insight, at best, or a moment of peace at least. A yantra is sort of a visual version of a mantra, a pattern or design that you concentrate upon while meditating. This is Jeffrey's.

There are five repeating blocks in this pattern; the block diagram shows where they all fall. Since blocks **A, B, E,** and **F** are variations of each other, you will find that the same templates can be used in several blocks. The tricky thing about this pattern is that so many pieces in it are mirror images of each other (see p. 38). To avoid confusion, be sure that you mark each template on both sides *as you make it.* One might say *#3, Block* **A,** and *#2, Block* **B** on one side and *#6, Block* **A,** and *#4, Block* **B** on the other.

This pattern is a regular carnival of long diagonal seams. They can be difficult because they tend to stretch. You must also be careful in laying them up (see p. 45 for a review of test-basting).

109

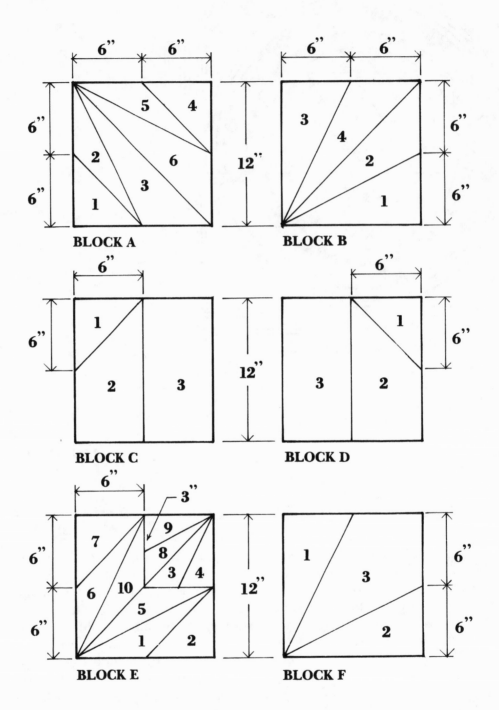

ASSEMBLY DIAGRAM

	A	A	B	B	A	A	
A	B	C	C	D	D	B	A
A	D	F	E	E	F	C	A
B	D	E	E	E	E	C	B
B	C	E	E	E	E	D	B
A	C	F	E	E	F	D	A
A	B	D	D	C	C	B	A
	A	A	B	B	A	A	

PIECING

Block **A**

Test-baste **1** to **2.** Sew and press.
Test-baste **1–2** to **3.** Sew and press. Repeat for other half of block. Join center diagonal. (Keep in mind that **4, 5,** and **6** are the mirrors of **1, 2,** and **3.**)

Block **B**

Test-baste **1** to **2.** Sew and press. Repeat for **3** and **4.** Join center diagonal.

Blocks **C** and **D**

1. Sew **1** to **2.** Press.
2. Sew **1–2** to **3.** Press.

Block **E**

1. Test-baste **1** to **2.** Sew and press. Repeat for **6** and **7.**
2. Test-baste **3** to **4** and **8** to **9.** Sew and press.
3. Sew **3–4** to **5** and **8–9** to **10.** Press. Test-baste **1–2** to **5** and **6–7** to **10.** Sew and press. Join center diagonal.

Block **F**

Sew **1** to **2** to **3.** Press.

111

Wedding Chain

Size: 92″ × 104″ including 4″ borders
Sewing: easy
620 pieces: medium

Time was when every young bride received a wedding quilt from her friends and neighbors. The party at which it was planned was the forerunner of the bridal shower; in some areas the blushing bridegroom took a hand at designing an appliqué or quilting pattern for the quilt.

I designed this quilt to celebrate the marriage of two strong, unusual, and unsentimental people. It has two repeating blocks instead of one. I didn't mean anything in particular by that at the time, but it turns out that the quilt has now lasted approximately three times as long as the marriage did. Sometimes I think of usurping another old quilt name and changing this one to *Crosses and Losses,* except that the people involved appear unscathed and even enriched by their experiment.

PIECING

1. For block **A**, sew **1** to **2** (2×). Press. Sew **3** to **2** to **3** (2×). Press.
2. Sew **4** to **5** to **6** to **5** to **4.** Press. Join these three sections, basting at the joints. Press.
3. For block **B**, sew **1** to **2** to **3** (4×). Press.

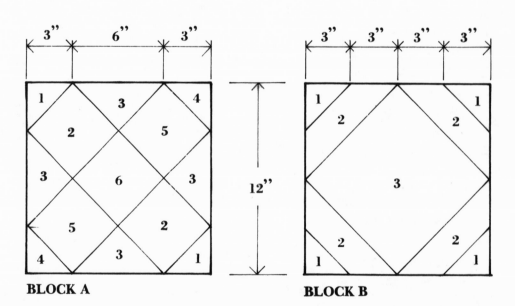

BLOCK A　　　　　**BLOCK B**

113

114

Amber Waves

Size: 90″ × 108″
Sewing: difficult
176 pieces: short

In piecework a major design consideration is the interplay between foreground and background. We have strived for designs in which parts of the foreground dissolve into the background, and others in which there is a positive-negative effect so that the background in one block is the foreground in the next. At last Jeffrey has managed to design a quilt in which part of the background drops off altogether. The design consists of a medallion of very simple blocks, then a border of arcs appliquéd onto background squares, and outside, a border in which the same arcs appear not appliquéd to anything.

PIECING

1. Test-baste **1** to **2.** Sew and press. Test-baste **2** to **3.** Sew and press.
2. Sew **1–2–3** to **4.** Press. Repeat for bottom half of block. Sew center seam, pinning at the joint.

BORDER UNITS

To make templates for the borders, measure and cut two 9½″ poster-board squares (9″ plus ¼″ margins all around). One

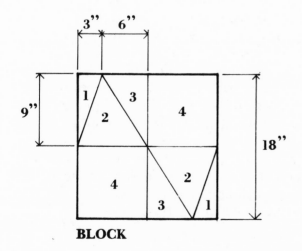

BLOCK

is for the background squares in the border **1** blocks. The second is to be cut to form templates **a** and **b**. To make **a** and **b**, measure and mark on the template the true corners of the block ¼″ in from the seam-margin edges (see diagram). The arc dividing **a** and **b** must go through the true corners, not through the corners of the seam margins. Use a string and pencil compass (see p. 70). Draw the arc as shown, and cut carefully on the curve line.

When you use these templates, trace with pencil on the wrong side of the fabric around all edges. Then cut directly on the drawn lines for the straight edges, which already have seam margins added to them, but cut *outside* the curved edge by ¼″, leaving the extra to turn under for the hem.

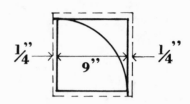

BORDER 1 UNITS

For the inner border, you need 32 border **1** units.

1. Trace and cut 32 background squares. Trace and cut 32 **b** shapes in the appropriate colors.
2. Baste **b** to the background square, with the straight edges matching.
3. Turn under the hem margin of the arc, pin it, and stitch it in place with invisible hand hemming stitches (see p. 53).

When all the units are completed, sew them into strips of eight, following the line drawing to get the orientation of the arcs right. Sew two strips to the sides of the medallion, matching and pinning the joints. Then add the remaining strips across top and bottom.

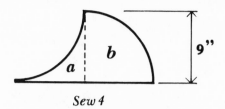

Sew 4

OUTER BORDER ENDS

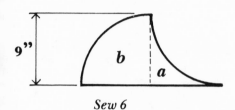

Sew 6

OUTER BORDER SIDES

Figure 1

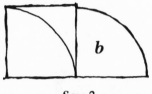

Sew 2

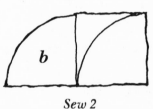

Sew 2

Figure 2

THE OUTER BORDER

1. Make eight border **1** units, two for each corner, as described above, and set aside until instruction 4.
2. Sew **a** to **b** as shown in figure 1, 4× for the ends, 6× in mirror image for the sides.
3. Sew **ab** to the four sides of the quilt top in the places indicated on the drawing, basting at appropriate joints. Begin and end each seam with a knot or backstitching ¼" from the raw edge of **ab.**

4. Sew **b** to border **1** units, as shown in figure 2. Join these pieces to the sides, as indicated in the line art. Leave ¼" free at each end of the seam. Lock with knot or backstitch.

5. Join the remaining pieces as shown as figure 3. Sew them in the appropriate places at top and bottom corners. Baste at all joints, and leave ¼" free at inside edges.

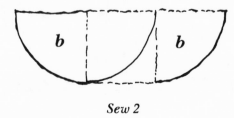

Sew 2

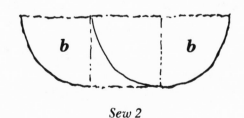

Sew 2

Figure 3

FINISHING THE EDGES

Piece a backing 90″ × 108″. Assemble the three layers of the quilt as usual, but trim the back and batting to match the edges of the top. After quilting, you might finish one of two ways. The easiest would be to turn the edges of the top and of the backing in toward the center of the quilt. Pin heavily, especially around the curves, easing as you go to keep the arcs smooth. Whip the edges together by hand, or topstitch by machine.

Your second choice, probably the most elegant, is to bind off with bias strips of fabric. Bias strips stretch and thus fit easily around curves and corners. To cut on the bias, fold a corner of the fabric you are going to use so that the selvedge forms a right angle, as shown. Press. Cut off the corner. The resulting diagonal edge, which should form a 45° angle with the selvedge, is now on the bias, and you have only to cut strips parallel to it. Cut the strips ¾″ to 1″ wide and keep piecing them together until you have enough to surround the quilt. Then bind off as usual: Sew the tape to the right side of the quilt, through all layers, by hand or machine, with a ¼″ seam. Turn the tape to the back of the quilt, enclosing the raw edge; turn under a narrow hem and hand-stitch with an invisible hemming stitch.

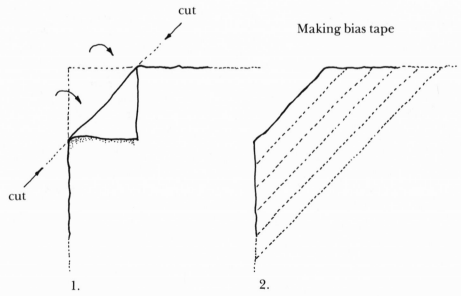

cut

cut

Making bias tape

1.

2.

left: *Winter Pine,* by Molly Upton, 1974 (83″ × 74″)
right: *Hourglass Infinity,* by Susan Hoffman, 1974 (82″ × 75″)

Road to Oklahoma City

Size: 84″ × 96″ plus border or binding
Sewing: medium
514 pieces: medium

This design is made with a traditional block called *Road to Oklahoma.* I was in Oklahoma City awhile back to give a seminar, and I met a number of people who had learned to make quilts when Oklahoma was still a territory. Some friends of the art center where I was speaking took me out to dinner; both had been children of pioneers and had walked miles to one-room schoolhouses, and my host was one-sixteenth Osage Indian. This was significant because the particular desolate corner of the territory that had been assigned to the Osages turned out to be floating on oil. Each year my host was allowed to cast one-sixteenth of a ballot at the tribal elections and received one-sixteenth of a share of the tribe's income. They took me to a restaurant at the top of a column-shaped building. The restaurant went all around the rim of the building, and all during dinner it rotated slowly, giving a view for twenty miles in all directions. I adjusted to rotating after a while, and dinner was very exciting because everything they brought me to eat was on fire, even the ice cream. If you're ever in Oklahoma City and want to have ice cream that's on fire, order Bananas Foster.

All the pieced blocks in this quilt are the same, but some are rotated to go in the opposite direction from the others. The sewing itself is very easy, but I graded it medium because the organization is a little unusual. The only remotely difficult thing about the construction is that you will have to cut out four 18″ squares of background fabric (see #3, assembly diagram). Use a yardstick and a right angle or large T square to be sure you have the squares square.

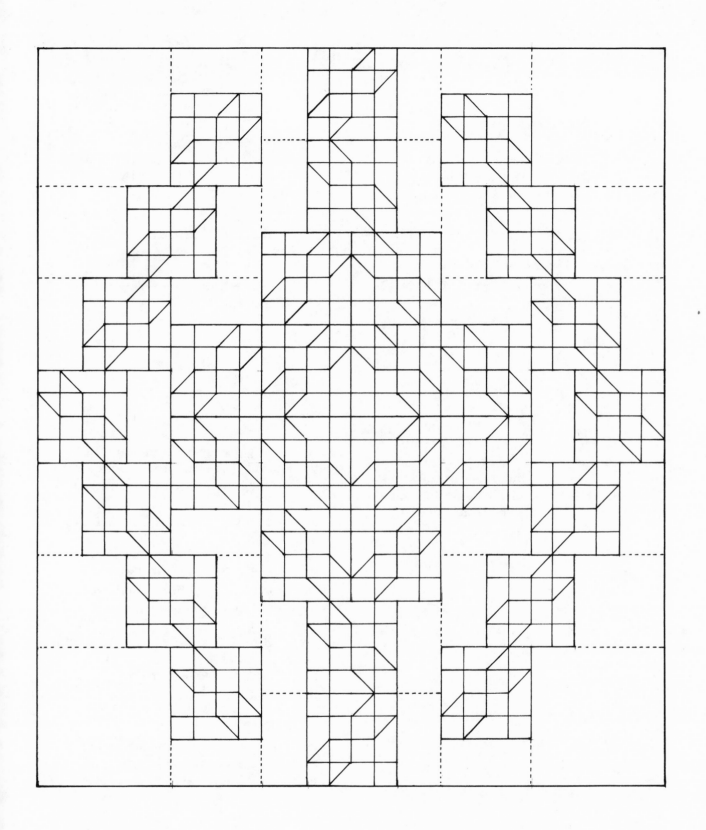

PIECING

First, cut and sew the 30 pieced blocks. Notice that trapezoids **2** and **5** are mirror images of each other. Take appropriate care during cutting (see p. 38).

1. Sew **1** to **2** and **3** to **4** (2×). Press and sew **2** to **3** (2×). Press.

2. Sew **5** to **6** (2×) and **7** to **8** (2×). Press and sew **5–6** to **7–8** (2×), basting at joints. Sew **7–8** to **7–8**. Press.

3. Sew **1–2–3–4** to side of **5–6–7–8** (2×). Press.

ASSEMBLING THE TOP

First, cut out the solid background pieces. You will need four 18½" squares (18" plus ¼" margins all around), four 12½" squares, and 26 rectangles 12½" × 6½". Make a template as usual for the rectangle. For the larger squares you can draw the shape once carefully on fabric with yardstick and right angle, then cut out and trace the other three from the first.

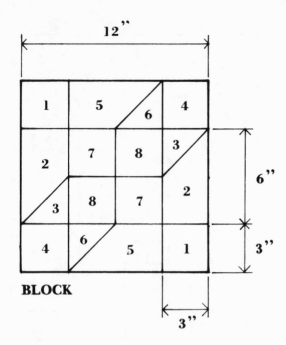

BLOCK

The top goes together in columns. The shaded squares represent pieced blocks. Refer to the line diagram to be sure you have the blocks turned in the right direction.

1. Sew **1–2** to **3** (4×). Press and sew **1–2–3** to **4–5–6** (4×). That completes the four corner areas (**A**).

2. Sew **7–8** (6×). Sew **9** to **10** (4×). Be sure to refer to the line art often to make sure you have the blocks going in the right directions.

3. Sew **7–8** to **8–7** to **7–8** (2×). Sew **9–10** to **10–9** (2×). Press.

4. Sew **7–8–8–7–7–8** to **9–10–10–9** (2×) to complete the sections labeled **B**. Sew **A** to **B** to **A** (2×).

5. Assemble column **C** as shown in the chart, checking often against the line art. Finally, sew the long seams that join the three columns, pinning at every joint. Press.

Fanfare, by Molly Upton, 1975 (78″ × 117″)

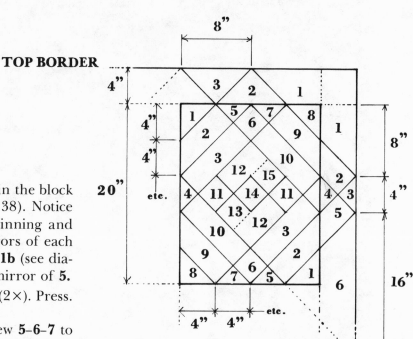

TOP BORDER

BLOCK

SIDE BORDER

PIECING

Before you cut, notice that **2** in the block is a mirror image of **9** (review p. 38). Notice also that the **1** shapes at the beginning and end of each border strip are mirrors of each other. Cut four as **1a** and four as **1b** (see diagram). In the side border, **2** is a mirror of **5**.

1. For the block, sew **1** to **2** to **3** (2×). Press. Sew **4** to **3** (2×). Press.
2. Sew **5** to **6** to **7** (2×). Press. Sew **5–6–7** to **1–2–3–4** (2×). Press.
3. Sew **8** to **9** to **10** (2×). Press.
4. Sew **11** to **12** (2×). Press. Sew **13** to **14** to **15**. Press.
5. Sew **11–12** to **13–14–15** (2×), pinned at joints, to form center square. Press.
6. Sew **8–9–10** to center square (2×). Press.
7. Sew remaining pieced areas in place, as indicated in the diagram, pinning at all joints. Press.

Piece the top and bottom border in continuous strips.

To piece the side border, test-baste and sew **1** to **2** (see p. 45). Press and add **3**. Sew **4** to **5**. Test-baste and sew **4–5** to **6**. Press. Sew **1–2–3** to **4–5–6**, basting at the joint. Press, and complete the strip in like manner.

Board Meeting

Size: 72″ × 84″, including 8″ plain border
Sewing: medium
305 pieces: quick

This pattern has been named *Board Meeting* because it was in fact devised at a board meeting. Unless you piece by hand, patchwork is not so easy to tote around with you as other kinds of needlework, but making up patchwork designs is a superior form of doodling that can be practiced anywhere. In fact, it's a great aid to concentration. If you are really serious, you can take graph paper and colored pencils to meetings with you.

The block in this quilt is a rectangle instead of a square. I think it came out that way because the opposing factions at the meeting were not quite evenly matched.

125

126

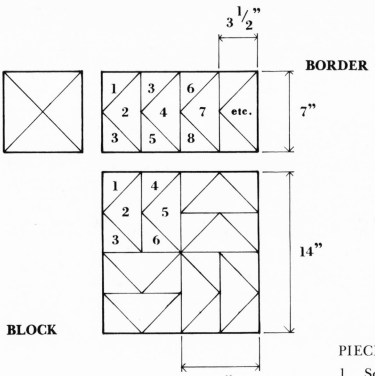

BORDER

3 ½"

7"

BLOCK

7"

14"

PIECING

1. Sew **1** to **2** to **3** and press. Sew **4** to **5** to **6** and press. Sew **1–2–3** to **4–5–6.** Press.
2. Repeat for other quadrants and join them as the diagram indicates. Pin at the center joint.

Piece the side strips of the inner border first, then sew them in place with a pin at each joint. Piece the top and bottom strips of the inner border, with the appropriate corner square at each end. Pin and sew. Measure and cut 7"-wide plain strips. Pin the side strips first with a pin every 3". Sew, press, and add end strips across top and bottom. Make the outer pieced border as you did the inner one.

Wild Goose Chase

Size: 84" × 98"
Sewing: easy
720 pieces: substantial

This is a very traditional sort of pattern. It is called *Wild Goose Chase* because the triangles in the borders suggest birds in formation, flying south for the winter (I always think). Triangles in piecework often represented birds. In their indispensable book *Quilts in America,* Patsy and Myron Orlofsky point out that there were many patterns named after birds, flowers, butterflies, trees, fruits, and seeds, but none named for vegetables. I've been thinking about that ever since I read it, and I can't make anything of it at all.

Kaleidoscope

Size: 90″ × 90″ including 3″ borders
Sewing: medium
588 pieces: medium

As you can see from the diagrams, this quilt has four simple repeating blocks. Block **A,** the main block, is a traditional one called *Tippecanoe,* named after General Harrison's victory over some Indians in 1811 at the Tippecanoe River. He later made a successful run for the presidency on the slogan "Tippecanoe and Tyler Too"; people used to put a lot of stock in campaign phrases they could dance to.

Now that I think of it, the **B** blocks (which bisect the quilt vertically and horizontally) were inspired by the border of a quilt made for the duke of Wellington in 1813. I wonder why I didn't call the quilt *Old Soldiers Never Die.*

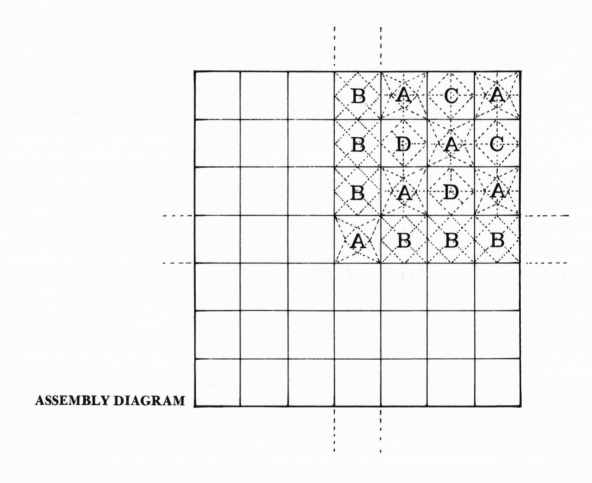

ASSEMBLY DIAGRAM

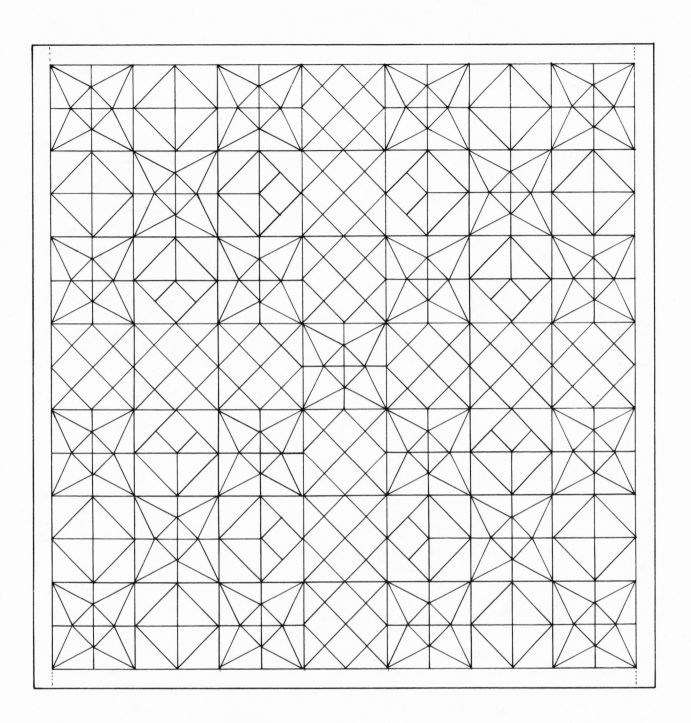

129

PIECING

Block **A** is, of course, a four-patch with four identical sections. Note that **2** and **3** are mirror images of each other (see p. 38).

1. Test-baste and sew **2** to **1** (see p. 45 about test-basting). Press. Test-baste and sew **3** to **1.** Press. Sew **4** to **1.** Press.
2. Repeat for other three quadrants and join them to form the block, basting at joints. Press.

Block **B**
1. This too is a four-patch. Sew **1** to **2** to **1** (4×). Press.
2. Join four sections, basting at all joints. Press.

Block **C**
Sew **1** to **2** (4×). Press and join four quadrants.

Block **D**
1. Sew **1** to **2** (2×).
2. Sew **3** to **4** to **3.** Press. Sew **5** to **3–4–3** (2×). Press.
3. Sew **1–2** to **1–2.** Press. Sew remaining vertical seam, basting at joint. Press.

ASSEMBLY

As you can see from the assembly diagram on p. 128, the blocks are arranged in four identical sections of **A, C,** and **D** blocks, divided by strips of **B** blocks, with one *Tippecanoe* (**A** block) in the center. First assemble each of the corner sections; then join the **B** blocks into four rows of three each. Then sew the left corner section to the **B** strip; then add the right corner section. Sew the middle strip **BBBABBB.** Sew the bottom as you did the top; then join the three sections—top, middle, bottom—basting at all joints.

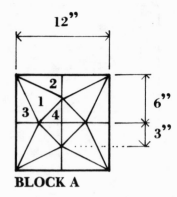

BLOCK A

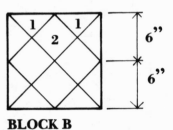

BLOCK B

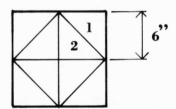

BLOCK C

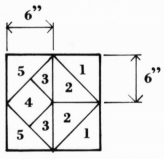

BLOCK D

Clay's Choice by Jeffrey Gutcheon, 1972 (32″ × 45″)

Other Kinds
of Quilts

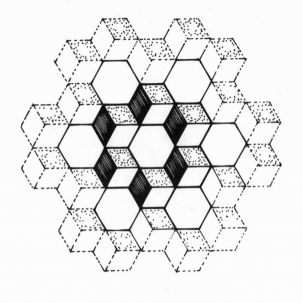

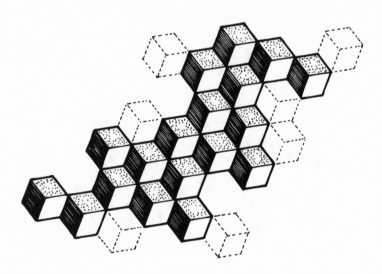

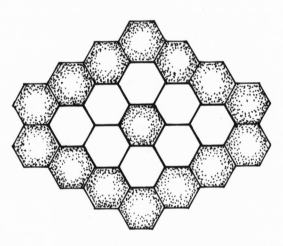

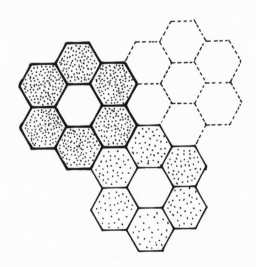

29. Sample shadings of hexagons and 60°-120° diamonds

ONE-PATCH PATTERNS

A one-patch pattern is a design that consists of only one geometrical element of a single size and shape. The pattern is created by manipulating the colors of the fabrics; one- and two-patch patterns are most commonly used in European patchwork, although they have also been popular in America.

One-patch piecework is usually planned to have a repeating pattern of darks and lights, but using many different fabrics instead of a controlled palette of four or five fabrics only. For that reason they make ideal scrap quilts. It's possible to make one-patch designs out of pentagons, octagons, triangles, and squares, but the most popular American versions use diamonds and/or hexagons.

HEXAGONS AND DIAMONDS

A diamond has four equal sides and two pairs of equal angles. A hexagon has six equal sides and six 120° angles. A hexagon can be divided into three equal diamonds, each having two 120° angles and two 60° angles. This sort of diamond makes the famous *Baby Blocks* or *Tumbling Block* pattern; if you group the diamonds in threes, shaded dark, medium, and light, you create a three-dimensional effect as if the blocks were projecting from the surface of the patchwork. You can make patterns with 60°–120° diamonds alone or with hexagons alone, or you can combine the two. We have given you here several sample shadings of the hexagons and diamonds used alone and together, and on p. 137 you have a sheet of hexagons and diamonds to color in as you like.

PIECING ONE-PATCH PATTERNS

Unlike most of the other patchwork in this book, these designs cannot by any finagling be made to go together with straight seams. They must be set together tightly and accurately, each corner sharp and precise, each angle accepting the corner exactly. Traditionally, they are pieced by hand using a special two-step process that insures that the pieces will all fit together with no gaps or puckers.

These patterns can be sewn on the machine if you are very skillful, but I don't see the point. If you are determined to sew by machine, choose a pattern that suits the technique. When I first began to make quilts, I did all piecing by machine because I was often unhappy in those days and consequently in a great hurry. I learned that patchwork can be more than the sum of its pieces when a neighbor invited me to join a group of her friends who were doing patchwork together. Through one winter we met one evening a week, exchanged scraps and some talk, cut and sewed our silent stitches for a hexagon quilt top while someone read aloud *Pride and Prejudice*. I don't remember how the quilt came out, and I don't much care. I remember those long, sweet evenings.

MAKE A MASTER TEMPLATE

First make poster board cutting templates as usual, but do not add seam margins. If you want to use the piece in one of the sizes we have drawn, simply trace the shape out of the book onto tracing paper. Then transfer the tracing to poster board by going over the lines again with a piece of carbon paper between the drawing and the poster board.

If you want to make the template larger or smaller than what we have drawn, you can construct them yourself with a protractor, if you remember your geometry, or you can trace the angles out of the book and measure the sides between them to the size you want. As long as the angles are rendered exactly, the sides may be any length you like. They must, of course, be equal.

MAKE PAPER SEWING FORMS

Next, trace and cut out a number of paper templates exactly the same as the master cardboard template. Christmas cards or heavy grocery bags are the right weight paper. Cut out a piece of fabric by eye, at least ¼″ larger all around than the paper template (it doesn't have to be precise). Pin the paper template to the wrong side of the fabric patch, turn hem margins in over the sides of the paper (taking care to preserve the edges and angles perfectly), and sew the hems in place, using long basting stitches through all three layers of fabric and paper.

WHIP THEM TOGETHER

When you have prepared a number of patches in this way, sew them together, taking fine invisible whipstitches or hemming stitches through the edges. When a patch is completely set into the patchwork, with another patch permanently sewn in place on all its sides, you can cut and pull out the basting thread. The paper template will drop out, and if it has been handled carefully, it can be used again several times.

136

30. Diamond-hexagon pattern to color

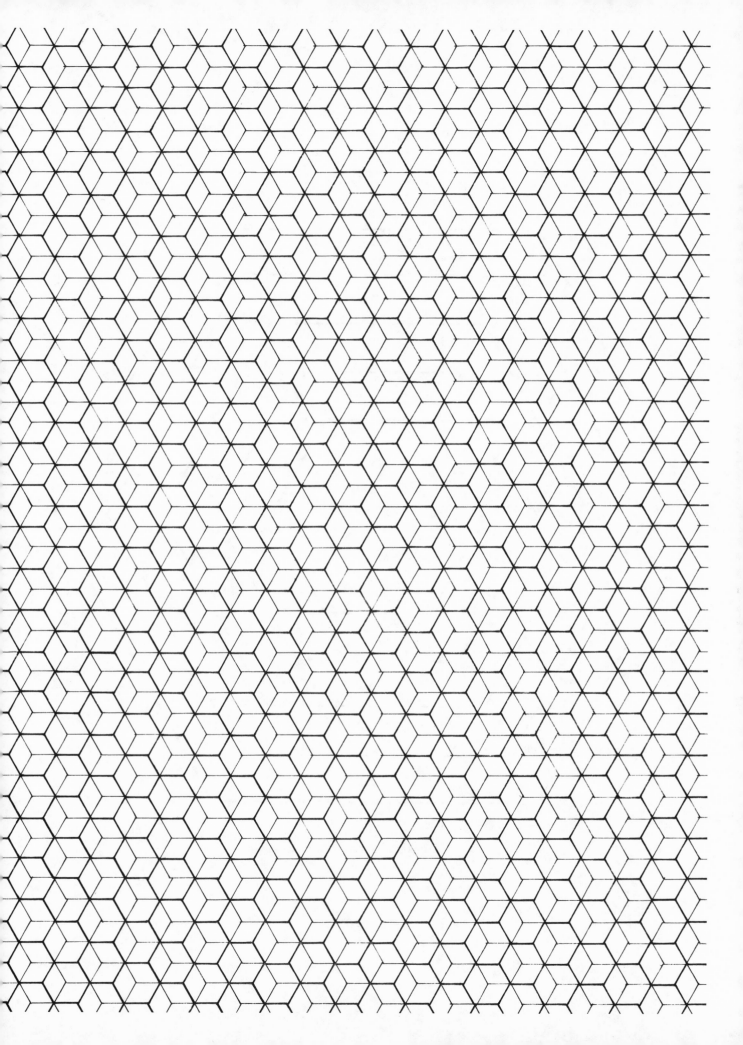

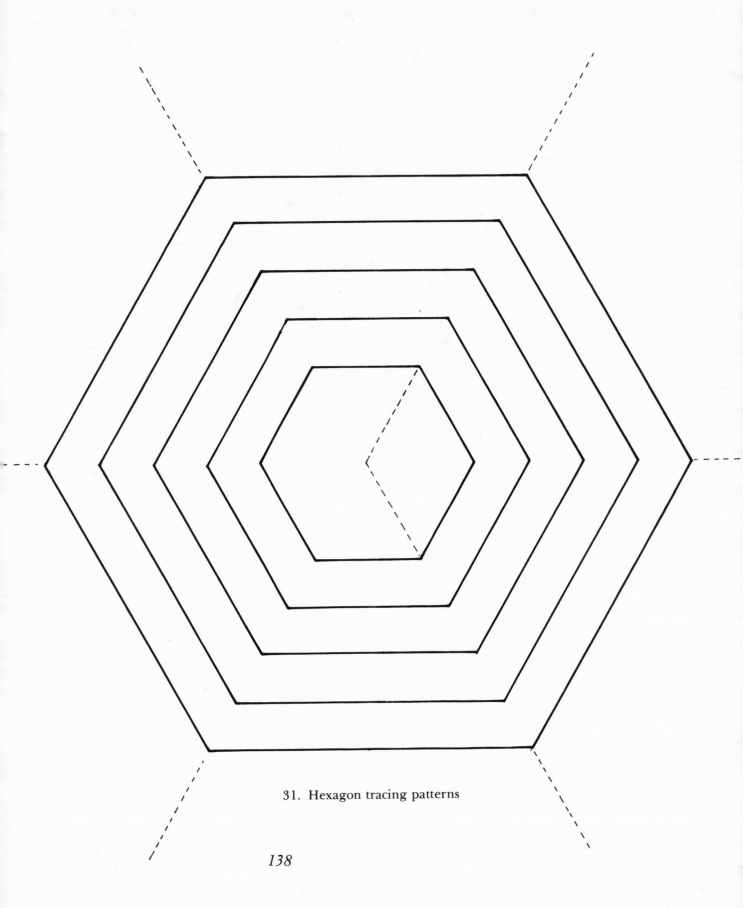

31. Hexagon tracing patterns

138

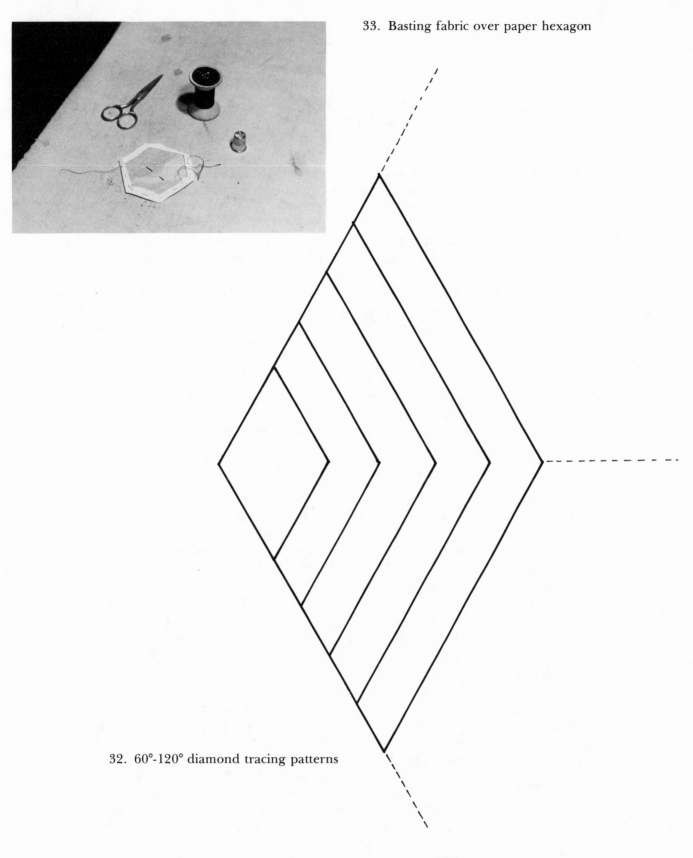

33. Basting fabric over paper hexagon

32. 60°-120° diamond tracing patterns

THE 45°–135° DIAMOND

This is probably the most versatile and popular American one-patch pattern of all. It can be used to make enormous Blazing Stars that cover a whole quilt top, or small repeating star blocks, or a large or small *Sunburst* pattern that can continue to radiate more or less indefinitely. As in the *Blazing Star* pattern shown here, you can divide a large diamond into four equal small ones or even nine equal small ones. Or combine diamonds of two different sizes to make a pattern like *Dove in the Window*. As with the 60°–120° diamond, you can make your own templates in any size you like by tracing the angle out of the book while measuring the sides to the length you choose.

You can square off a small Blazing Star to make a block by setting triangles into the sides and squares into the corners. These blocks can later be pieced together as usual. If you prefer, you can appliqué a Sunburst or some Blazing Stars onto larger expanses of quilt top, and this gives you more freedom to compose a large pattern.

Patterns using this diamond can be pieced as usual, by hand or machine, using straight seams in the order shown in the piecing diagram. If you prefer, you can piece by hand, using the paper-template method described above.

LOG CABIN PATTERNS

Log Cabin patterns were very popular in the nineteenth century, from about 1840 on. After the home sewing machine became common, they were often pieced by machine. Since the underneath side of this pattern is a thicket of seam margins, and since the more layers of fabric you have, the more difficult quilting becomes, these patterns were often not quilted. Instead, the layers were tacked with little hidden stitches in the corners of the blocks. In other cases they were fastened with knots made from decorative silk thread in the center of the squares, the tails of the knots left dangling. They were also made of wools, silks, and velvets on occasion.

There are two basic ways to shade this block. One is to have dark and light strips on opposite sides of the block, as on p. 145, and the other is to have dark strips on two adjacent sides and light strips on the remaining two sides. The overall pattern of the quilt top is created by turning the blocks in various directions to make the dark strips march across the quilt or go in circles or make zigzags or whatever. We've given you two traditional sample figures, and others are possible. If you want to save yourself coloring in the blocks over and over, you could

34. 45°–135° pattern to color

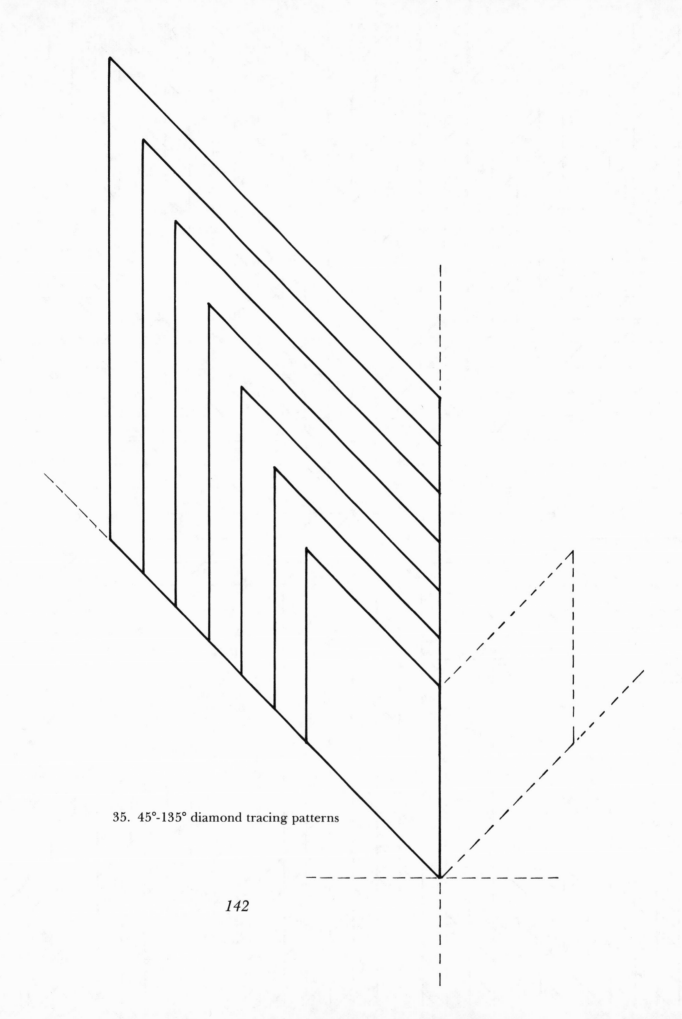

35. 45°-135° diamond tracing patterns

36a. *Sunburst*

36b. *Blazing Star*

36c. *LeMoyne Star*

36d. *Dove in the Window*

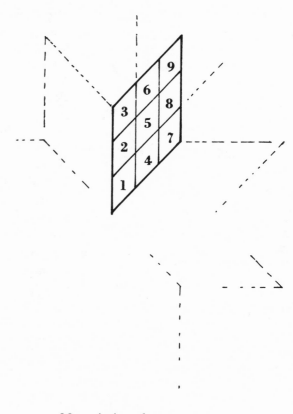

36e. piecing chart

color the blocks once on tracing paper as usual, cut them apart, and rearrange them as often as you like.

A word of caution. These quilts were sometimes done in two colors only, such as red and white, but more often they used a variety of materials. The traditional effect of the pattern absolutely requires that there be a high contrast between the light part and the dark part. That means that you cannot take all the scraps in your bag, sort them into relatively light or dark piles, and use them all; you can only use the ones that are really light or really dark. Medium colors cannot be persuaded to look lighter or darker than they are, and if you use them, the line of the pattern will melt into a mélange of motley. You may very well choose deliberately to allow the contrast between light and dark to dissolve in parts of the pattern while holding firm in others. That's very effective when done well, but very disappointing when done by mistake.

The *Log Cabin* is built on a foundation square of muslin. On the block showing the piecing order we have superimposed a scale to show you how to determine the size of each piece. If you count each square on the scale as 1″, as we recommend, the block will finish 8″ square, which is, to my mind, the most effective size for this pattern, but if you like, you can make it 12″ square instead by counting each square on the grid as 1½″.

Make templates as usual, with ¼″ seam margins all around. Cut a foundation square of muslin the size of the finished block plus ¼″ all around. Fold this square in half diagonally (from corner to corner), then in half again, and press with a hot iron. Unfold the square, which will now have creases from corner to corner that cross exactly in the center of the block.

Pin the small square patch to the center of the quilt, with each corner on a crease. Lay piece 2, right sides together, along the top of 1, and sew by hand or machine through all three layers (2, 1, and background muslin), as shown. Open 2 out into place and press. Now lay on 3, right sides together across 1 and 2, matching edges carefully. Stitch, open, and press. Continue building the square in this way, proceeding clockwise around the block until all the strips have been sewn in place and pressed. When you have sewn all the blocks in this manner, assemble the blocks into rows, taking a ¼″ seam as you would with any other quilt top.

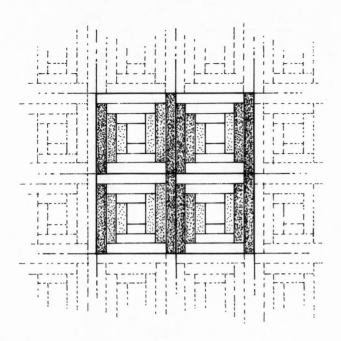

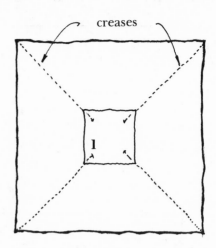

39a. muslin square creased;
1 pinned in center

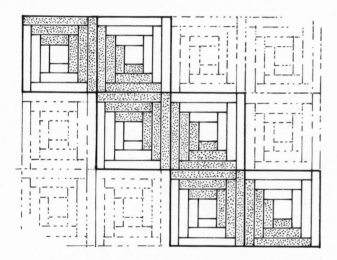

37. *Log Cabin* sample shadings

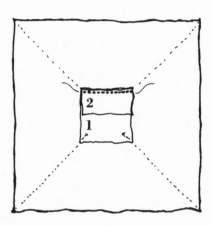

39b. **2** sewn in place

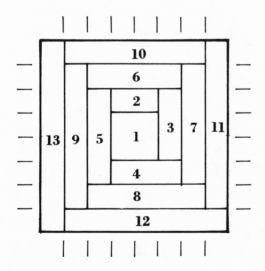

38. *Log Cabin* piecing chart

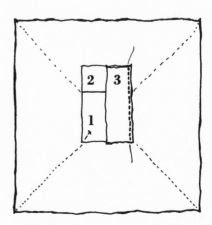

39c. **2** opened out, **3** basted in place

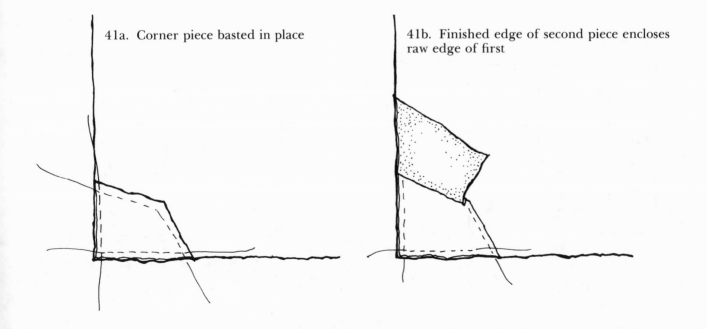

36" x 4"

18" x 18"

36" x 36"

40. Diagram of crazy quilt background

41a. Corner piece basted in place

41b. Finished edge of second piece encloses raw edge of first

IX. *Refractions* (48″ × 60″), an
unquilted top by Jeffrey Gutcheon

X. *The Star Also Rises* (100″ × 100″)
by Beth Gutcheon

XI. *Mirrored Squares and Triangles*
(71″ × 71″) by Susan Hoffman

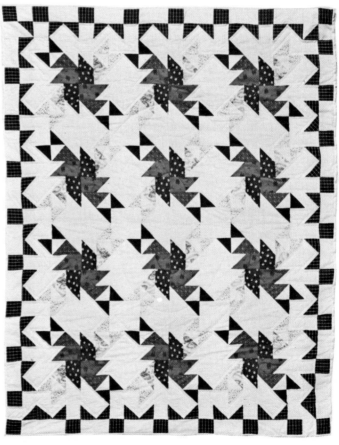

XII. *Rolling Pinwheel* (52″ × 68″)
by Beth Gutcheon

XIII. *Checkerboard Skew* (52″ × 72″)
by Beth Gutcheon

XIV. *Night and Day* (54″ × 78″)
by Jeffrey Gutcheon

XV. *Katherine Wheels* (72″ × 90″)
by Beth and Jeffrey Gutcheon

XVI. *David's Quilt* (58″ × 66″)
by Beth and Jeffrey Gutcheon

CRAZY QUILTING

Crazy quilting is built up on foundation sheets of muslin as *Log Cabin* blocks are. The surface is crazy as in crazed or cracked glass or ice, not as in cuckoohaha. The patchwork itself is determined as you go, not designed beforehand, but the overall surface of many quilts has a subtle graphic organizing principle. The crazed patchwork may be built on a series of squares, all the same size, or centered around a large medallion area with smaller squares and rectangles around it, or juxtaposed with "straight" areas of piecework, appliqué, or plain fabric.

Plan a large patchwork pattern for the background pieces, such as the one shown, and cut out muslin foundation pieces to correspond to the measurements you have worked out, leaving ¼" seam margins all around. Cover the entire surface of each background piece as follows:

Start in the corner of the muslin, with a patch cut in a right angle, as shown. You can use silks, velvets, velveteens, corduroys, or whatever fabric you like for this patchwork if you don't plan to wash or quilt it. Baste the corner piece in place. Choose or cut another scrap, usually one that contrasts in size, shape, color, texture, or all of the above. Lay it right sides together at the edge of the first piece, and sew it in place by hand or machine through all three layers (two patches and the foundation muslin).

When you make this seam, which is permanent, sew only to within ¼" of the raw edge at each end, and knot or backstitch the thread to lock the seam. As far as possible you try to have the raw edge of each piece overlapped by the finished edge of the next one, but in the nature of this sort of pattern, there will also be edges that are not overlapped by anything. These must be turned under by hand and secured with temporary basting stitches. It is to make this turn-under possible that you leave the edges free at the end of each permanent seam. But do not leave any raw edges permanently. When the whole foundation area is covered, secure the basted hems with permanent decorative embroidery stitches, applied by hand or machine. Then remove the basting.

This much embroidery is functional and necessary, but in Victorian crazy quilts there is often embroidery decorating every seam whether it is needed to hold the patches in place or not. The embroidery can be very fancy, but it doesn't have to be. Any topstitch, machine or hand zigzag, or the like will do the job. This is an ideal kind of patchwork to do with very small children.

When all the background pieces are patched and embroidered, sew them together by hand or machine, taking a ¼″ seam. If you like, you can finish by embroidering all the straight seams between the foundation pieces, especially if you want to call attention to them.

Only very rarely does such a quilt have a batting. If you want a sculptural effect (and a little extra warmth), you can stuff a tuft of batting under each patch as you are building the crazy work. When the top is finished, lay it together with a backing of your choice (consider corduroy, velveteen, or some other lush, heavy fabric) and secure the two layers with hidden tacks or with knots made with silk embroidery thread. Bind off as usual. If you have made an ornamental scalloped or jagged edge, bind off with bias tape (see p. 118).

APPLIQUÉ

Appliqué, as you probably know, is French for "applied," and it refers to applying little pieces to bigger ones. Every patch on the knee of your blue jeans is an appliqué. Appliqué as a quilt design tradition is different from piecework in that it is painterly rather than graphic, and it resembles collage, while piecework is like mosaic. The process is so different from that of piecework that it really might as well be a different craft.

Rather than providing a sheaf of ready-made appliqué designs for you to follow, we have offered here just a few suggestions for designing appliqué as an excuse to talk about the different attitudes and techniques you might bring into play in designing your own. If you want to faithfully reproduce traditional appliqué patterns, *The Standard Book of Quiltmaking* by Marguerite Ickes, available in paperback from Dover Press, has a complete assortment of Whig Roses, bows, swags, and other standard appliqué motifs to trace out and use.

SWALLOWS

Appliqué does sometimes use a repeating design unit, as piecework does. The design might be one simple motif applied to a background square, or it might be a complex assembly of, say, flowers, stems, and petals repeated identically in each block of the quilt. You can get such patterns from books, draw them freehand, or make them by cutting out a design from paper as you made snowflakes when you were a child.

I made this *Swallow* pattern by folding a piece of paper in half lengthwise and cutting out the silhouette of half the bird.

148

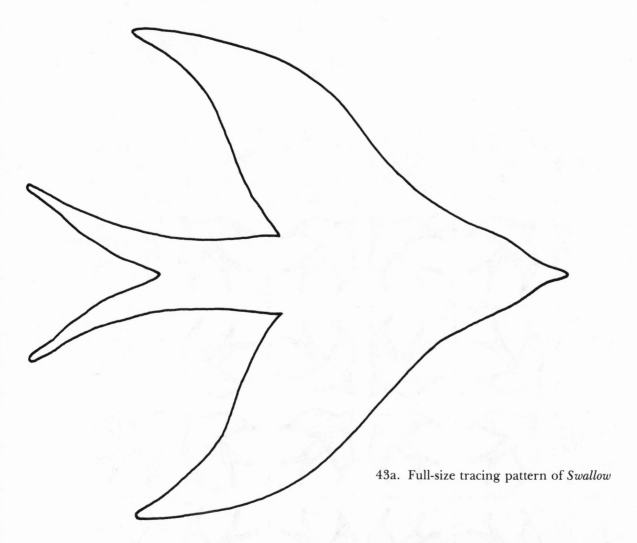

43a. Full-size tracing pattern of *Swallow*

42. *Genesis:* machine appliqué wall hanging
(32″ × 22″). Hand appliqué pillow (18″ × 18″).
By Virginia Avery

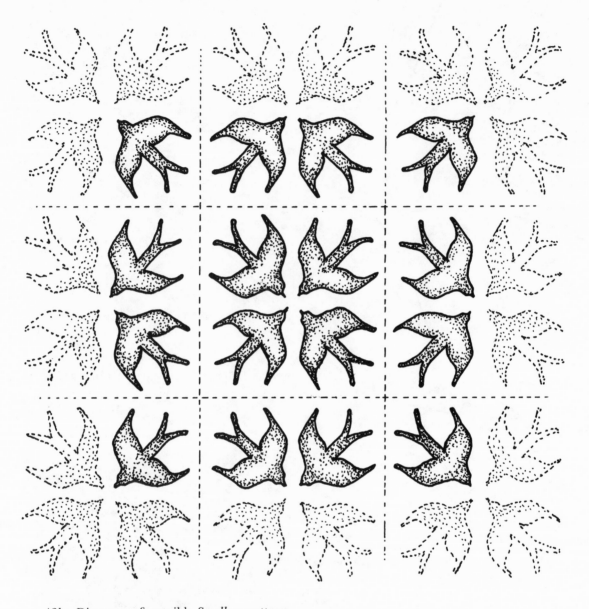

43b. Diagram of possible *Swallow* pattern

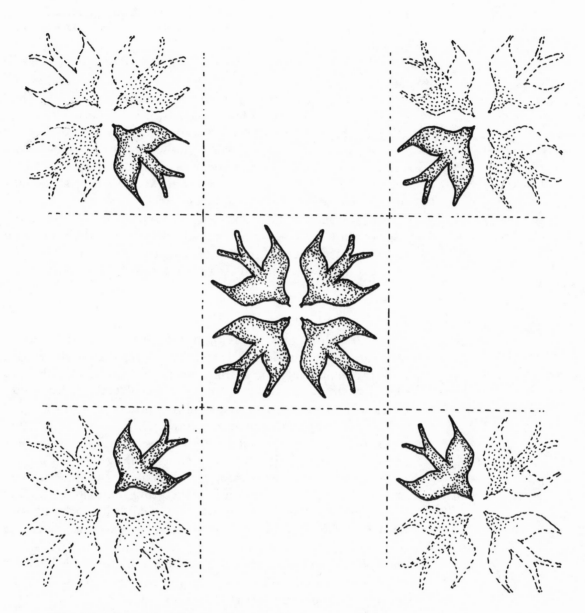

43c. Diagram of possible *Swallow* pattern

When I unfolded the paper, I had the whole bird, completely symmetrical. You can make more elaborate patterns by folding the paper in half diagonally (from corner to corner) and then in half again before you cut.

I chose the bird because it is versatile and illustrates several things at once. First, it is in fact a picture of a bird, and appliqué is especially good for representing pictures of things, while piecework is not, particularly. Second, it is also effective as an abstract shape. If you position four of them together nose to nose on a background square, as shown in the diagram, it does what I always like about good piecework design: It makes a series of compelling foreground shapes, and leaves an equally interesting negative pattern in the background.

If you position the birds straight up and down on the background square, as shown in the second diagram, you create a different foreground-background pattern; and if you combine the two, you will create yet a third.

SEWING APPLIQUÉ

The technique for making appliqué has everything to do with the way it is designed. Instead of fitting shapes into a rigid and invariable structure that must be completely planned ahead of time, an appliqué form can be placed on the design more or less wherever it looks right. You can move it around before you make a final decision about where it goes. Since that is one of appliqué's special qualities, it seems best to me to make the most of it and give yourself scope to design as you go.

When you are using a repeating shape in appliqué (as you are here), you make a poster board cutting template by tracing the shape onto tracing paper and then again with carbon paper onto the poster board. Do not add seam margins. Place the template on the wrong side of the fabric and trace the shape with pencil or chalk pencil. Cut out, leaving about a ¼″ margin all around, as shown, for a turn-under. Clip and notch the hem margin at angles and curves to allow it to be turned under smoothly. Be very careful not to cut beyond the pencil line. Pin the shape to the background fabric; turn under the hem margin and pin it. A tweezer used as tiny tongs helps in turning under. Sew the hem in place with invisible hemming stitches. (You can also use a machine topstitch, zigzag, or satin stitch.)

If you are sewing by hand, use a cotton thread to match the appliqué piece, and if you have trouble with the thread tying itself in knots, coat it with beeswax.

My problem with designing appliqué is that I can't draw. I

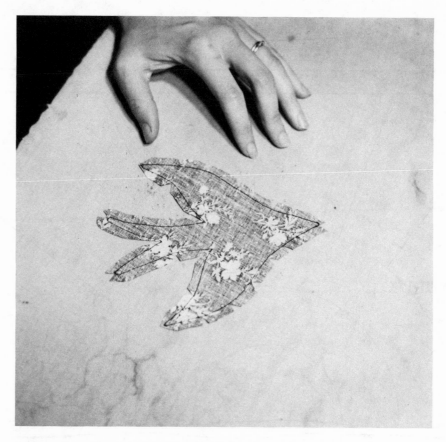

44. *Swallow* cut out, margins clipped and notched

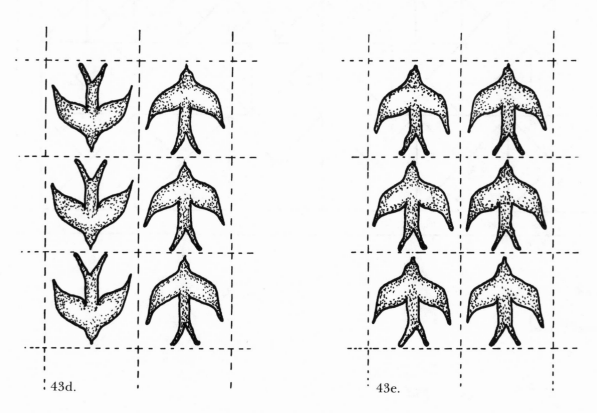

43d.   43e.

Diagrams of possible *Swallow* patterns

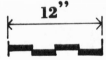

12"

45. *Once Is Not Enough*

154

can with perseverance make a pattern for this bird design, but if I were to try to draw a picture of the quilt I meant to make from it, it would end in despair. Instead, I plan the general geometric scheme of the piece in my head or on graph paper, with embarrassing little sketches and diagrams suggesting where I think the forms might be placed and in what direction they will be going.

I might decide to make this quilt with thirty repeating blocks all like diagram **a,** surrounded by a strip or two of diagram **b,** with the birds all flying in single file around the quilt. But more likely I would begin in the middle with four 12″ blocks like those in diagram **a,** then surround that with large blank rectangles with birds more widely spaced, then throw in a narrow strip with birds flying in single file all around the medallion, then insert some more widely spaced birds with perhaps some clouds or trees thrown in (or would these birds have laurel branches in their mouths?)—I wouldn't know until I cut out the shapes, pinned them to the background, and thought about how I liked it. Another possibility would be to apply each bird to a 6½″ square (6″ plus ¼″ seam margins all around) and then make a pattern out of them by spreading them on the floor and moving them around till I liked the motion and balance. I leave it to you.

PICTORIAL QUILTS
ONCE IS NOT ENOUGH

When I was at college, one of my friends had a room-and-board job living with a professor whose daughter had cerebral palsy. The daughter, confined to a wheelchair and unable to talk coherently, was bright and sensitive and literate, and she wrote beautiful letters. She did this by typing on an electric typewriter with a specially designed hat that had a long stiff peak because she had no control over any muscles except those in her neck. She could hit the keys with her pointed hat. Once my friend took the daughter home with her to Vermont for the weekend, where they gave her the first waffles of her life, took her to see her first skiing, and at her request woke her up at 5:00 in the morning because in nineteen years of life nobody had ever thought to get her up in time to see the sun rise.

Jeffrey has designed these pictorial patterns to combine piecework and appliqué. This one will finish 60″ × 75″, and you can add borders to any size you like.

For the waves, make triangular templates as usual and piece them in strips. After the triangles there are strips about 2″

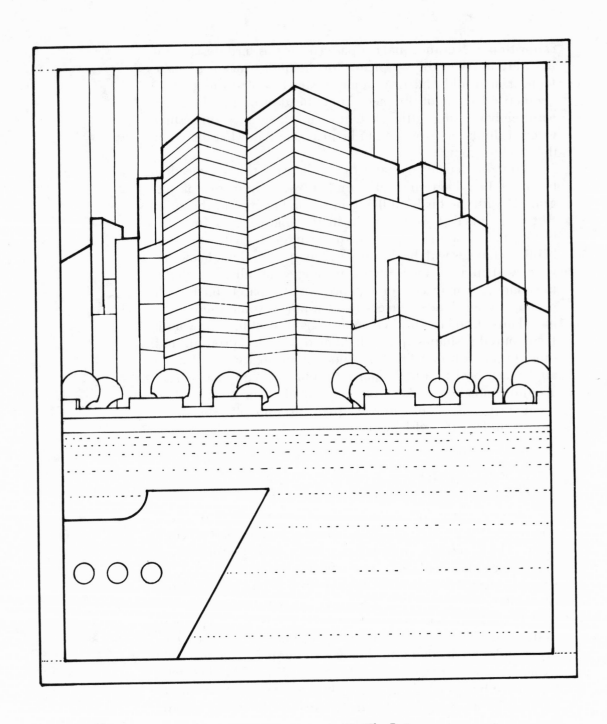

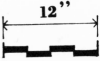 12"

46. *The Battery*

156

wide alternating light and dark areas to show light shining on the sea. They need not be exactly 2″ wide at all places, and in fact you might deliberately let the seams between them wander a bit. The total ocean area is then about 35″ high. The upper portion is about 40″ × 60″ and is probably made most easily by building on a foundation piece of muslin. Baste a stripe for the first sun's ray to the lower left corner of the foundation piece, matching the edges. Choose the next fabric, cut out roughly the size and shape you need, and sew it to the first piece, right sides together, through three layers (new piece, first piece, and background piece). This is the same technique as described for building crazy quilting. If necessary, finish trimming shape 2 so that the edges match the background piece and the width of the ray is what you want (it need not correspond to what we have drawn). Combine around to the last ray on the right, taking care that the raw edge of each piece is sewn down under the finished edge of the next one.

Next, cut and apply a series of arc shapes of diminishing sizes, ending with the semicircle in the middle of the sun. You can make these with a string-and-pencil compass or by tracing around round things like dinner plates, though I don't know what you will have around the house that's large enough for the outside one, unless it's your snow tires (see p. 70 about string-and-pencil compass). For that matter, feel free to cut the arcs by eye. They don't have to be perfect, and you may well prefer a little poetic license; that's what appliqué is good for. Notch the hem margins of the convex (outcurving) side of the largest arc and stitch it in place with invisible hemming stitches. This edge should cover and enclose all the raw edges of the ends of the rays. In the same fashion hem the convex edge of the next arc over the raw inner edge of the first one, and so on until the sun is completed. Sew the two halves of the quilt together by hand or machine.

THE BATTERY

If you like, you can piece this whole design, or you can make it by applying the building shapes to background strips left bare at the top to form part of the sky. Make the vertical building strips first. When you make the two main skyscrapers in the foreground, try keeping all the strips on the left side light and those on the right side dark to enhance the illusion that the buildings project out of the picture.

Next cut and sew horizontal strips in varying widths for the harbor and piece them with as wobbly a seam as you like. Since

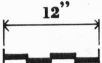

12"

47. *Pioneer Valley*

the upper strips are to be measured more by taste than inches, you won't know what width the whole medallion will finish till you have sewn the vertical strips together. Measure the horizontal strips to match whatever the top part came out to. Lap the bottom of the buildings over the top of the harbor, turn under the hems, and stitch in place. Cut out and appliqué a balustrade at the base of the building, then some round shapes representing trees, taxis, and so on. Add borders to whatever size you need.

PIONEER VALLEY

This is a picture of the part of Massachusetts where Jeffrey went to school. There are no more pioneers there.

Cut and piece strips of fabric of diminishing widths for the sky until you have an area about 40″ × 70″. Cut a piece of foundation muslin 30″ × 70″ on which to build the rest of the design and sew it to the bottom of the sky. Piece some patches, roughly square or oblong, to represent fields, and pin them into the bottom right of the foreground. For the area above the fields piece some strips herringbone fashion and pin them in place. Leave raw edges raw for the minute; you are still composing. In the left foreground you will need some wider striped pieces stretching from the lower left corner all the way to the sky. When these have been pieced together and pinned in place, choose the fabric that will form the river, lay it on the middle of the quilt overlapping both its banks, and begin to trim until you have cut it down to the shape you want plus a margin for turning under.

Next cut a shape roughly triangular for the smallest mountain, farthest in the background. Pin it in place, and if necessary, trim it to the right size and shape. Repeat for the rest of the mountains, building out toward the foreground. Last, cut out some curved tree or bushy shapes and pin them in place in the right foreground. Survey your work, and shift and trim until you find that it is good.

By hand or machine sew the raw edges of the fields on either side of the river to the foundation fabric. The seam between the checkerboard fields and the herringbone ones should be turned under and made by hand because it is a finished edge. Turn under and hem the banks of the river, enclosing underneath the raw edges and foundation stitching of the land on either side. Turn under and hem the sides of the mountains, starting with the one in the background and working forward. Finish the trees and bushes in the foreground and add borders to whatever size you need.

HOW TO DESIGN
A QUILTING PATTERN

Quilting, as I'm sure I've said before, is both decorative and functional. It must serve to hold the three layers in place and prevent them from shifting or lumping or bunching up. It also sinks down into the puffiness of the quilt and creates a bas-relief pattern, giving the quilt a depth and texture it wouldn't otherwise have. You have probably noticed that in traditional quilts, particularly the masterpiece versions that have survived in mint condition (because they were used very little), the quilting is applied with a pretty broad brush. Every inch tends to be filled with quilted scrolls and plumes and lover's knots. This is partly because the quilting did indeed add durability to the piece, but it was also, in part, a more existential statement of the value the maker put upon her own work, and indeed upon herself. By spending one hundred hours quilting a quilt when fifty would have worked, the quiltmaker created a permanent record of her skill and her patience and of her belief that persistence and ornament really matter.

Modern quilting design has changed fundamentally, for two reasons. First, modern quiltmakers believe that certain things really matter, but their beliefs are not so readily expressed by sheer quantity of quilting stitches. So the philosophical impetus for quilting every square inch is gone for most of us. At the same time, polyester batting, which holds together better than natural fibers because it is made in a sheet instead of bolls or handfuls, doesn't require nearly as much quilting as cotton or wool once did. The effect on design is this: Quilting designs were once superimposed on the patchwork patterns. The two were meant to harmonize; the vines and scrolls were planned to take advantage of blank spaces in the patchwork, but other than that the two often had nothing to do with each other, except in the case of outline quilting that followed the seams of the patchwork. But with outline quilting the tendency was to simply follow what was already there, not to minimize or maximize any elements in order to alter the emphasis of the patchwork design.

If you admire the old-style quilting patterns, you can get tracing templates for reproducing them exactly (see list of sources, p. 167). And there are certainly times when all you want to do by way of quilting is a dumb grid of crisscrossing straight lines. Sometimes that's what works best. But often it is possible to design a quilting pattern that actually heightens the effect of the patchwork by bringing out a movement or a symmetry or asymmetry that wasn't apparent before.

48a.

Diagrams of *Rolling Pinwheel* quilting patterns

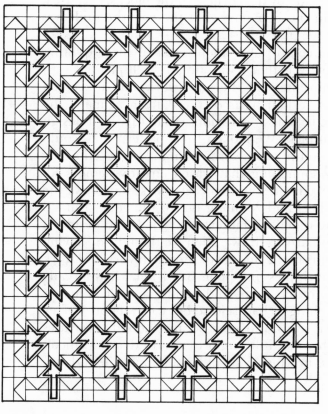

48b.

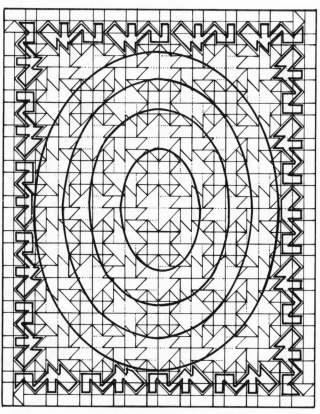

48c.

When planning a quilting pattern, I usually work with a piece of tracing paper over my colored-in diagram of the quilt top. Also, I usually take my sweet time about it; I like to have the quilt top on the wall for a while where I can ponder it before I decide about the patchwork pattern I want to emphasize.

We have shown you here three possible designs for *Rolling Pinwheel* and three for *The Star Also Rises*. When I'm thinking about what to quilt, the first thing I look for is something actually in the patchwork that is interesting but not obvious. Since in the nature of things the colored foreground elements usually catch the eye first, I look to see if there are interesting shapes in the background that are being overlooked. In example 1 for *Rolling Pinwheel,* I tried outlining the jagged blank spaces left between the colored pinwheels.

Next I tried outlining the pinwheels themselves, because they are the most important part of the foreground design. (I should probably call it "inlining" because I have the quilting fall inside the seams I want to call attention to.) The pinwheels are pieced from four separate trapezoids, but I wanted to outline the shape as a whole to see if that would add force or movement. Since that figure alone would not provide enough quilting to hold the batting together, I decided to emphasize the Greek-cross figure made by the corners of the blocks, because it was there, intact, in the geometry, but the way the quilt was colored you didn't see it.

I felt not quite comfortable about each of these quilting designs. The trouble was that I was already well pleased with the balance and movement of the patchwork, and it seemed when I emphasized certain parts of the pattern, it made the whole thing too predictable and obvious. So in the third design we tried a different tack: We looked for a pattern that would superimpose itself on the patchwork; it should be keyed to the patchwork but say something that wasn't already being said. First I thought of making a spiral on each block, starting at the center of the pinwheel and zooming out to the edge. But I'd already rejected the repetitive patterns I'd tried, and besides a spiral would be too hard to draw. Then we thought of having concentric circles start in the middle of the patchwork and work out to the edge like ripples in a pool. But I felt I had already used circles a lot in other quilts, and besides a circle is just as symmetrical as the things I had rejected already. Then Jeffrey suggested concentric ovals. I loved it because nobody ever uses ovals in quilts and because it brought to mind Edvard Munch's painting *The Scream,* in which a small person in a twilight landscape emits terrified soundless ovals that reverberate outward to the edges of the painting. So we put on ovals, and then around the edge we outlined the jagged white spaces where the blocks and the borders meet; this enclosed the ovals and provided the terror.

The pattern for *The Star Also Rises* presented a different problem since the patchwork itself was not repetitive. Here are three possible designs. The first follows the outlines of certain of the patchwork figures so as to emphasize the shapes left in the background when the different-size stars come together. This is the pattern I used.

Design 2 is Jeffrey's suggestion. He first conceived all the middle-size stars as forming a circle; then he encircled each star to make a circle of circles. The rest of the design echoes the original circles. The scalloped shapes on the small stars were suggested by what happened when we set up interior lines to echo the circles.

The third design first takes note of the axes created by the middle-size stars. Instead of seeing them as forming a circle, I saw them as forming a square on the diagonal, so I drew the line that made that point, letting it follow the outline of the star it reached at each of its corners. Then I made two lines parallel to the first, echoing inward. Then I decided to follow the diagonals formed by the points of the largest star leading out toward the corners of the quilt because that would create an **X** shape, roughly the opposite of the diagonal square. But I preserved the outline of the stars at the center and at the ends of the cross. Pentagons suggested themselves, so I put them in; then I had to add more quilting of some kind in the blank spaces, so I outlined the remaining stars.

HOW TO GET THE DESIGN ONTO THE TOP

Work on a hard flat surface, and mark with a regular pencil or with a chalk pencil. Make the lightest, finest line you can. When you are outlining a shape, have the line of quilting fall inside the seam by ¼″ or a little more so you won't have to quilt through any of the seam margins inside the patchwork. When you quilt through many layers of fabric, you find yourself forced to take longer stitches than usual, which looks messy, or else to take one stitch at a time, which takes a long time. Otherwise, you bend or break your needle.

49a.

49b.

Diagrams of *The Star Also Rises* quilting patterns

49c.

When you mark on an outline pattern, take care to have it parallel to the seam (see p. 32 for constructing parallels). A transparent ruler or T square with a grid printed on the plastic is a great aid for this; you can get such things at art-supply stores.

For long straight lines that do not follow a seam, use a yardstick as a guide.

To make a circle, tie a string to a sharp pencil, hold one end of the string at the center of the circle you want to draw, and have the point of the pencil at the place where you want the arc to fall. Swing the arc, keeping the string taut and the pencil straight up. (If you let the pencil lean, you effectively change the length of the string and allow the arc to wander off course.) That is the way to make large circles, and particularly to make circles that must be exactly the same size as something in the patchwork. If you are going to simply impose a series of circles over the blocks, you can trace around dinner plates or teacups.

To make an oval, you make a loop of string and place it over two focus points (I use pushpins), as shown. When you draw a pencil around the inside of the loop, pulling it taut all the way around, you get an oval. But the size and shape oval you get depends on where you put the two foci and how big the loop is, which you must determine hit or miss. That's why people don't use ovals in quiltmaking very much.

50. Oval being drawn

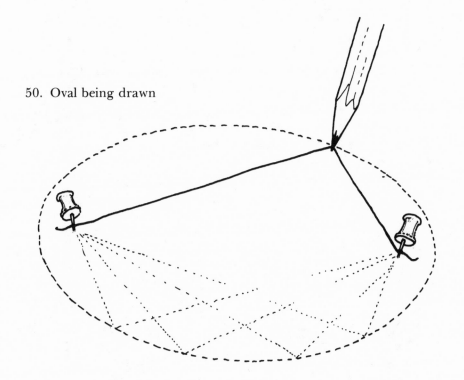

MAIL-ORDER RESOURCES
FOR QUILTMAKERS

Counterpane
P.O. Box 1567
Sausalito, Calif. 94965

A quilt gallery that buys and sells old and new quilts. To sell them yours, send them a picture of the quilt along with its dimensions and its price.

Country Peddler Quilt Shop
2242 Carter Ave.
St. Paul, Minn.

Cotton fabric, quilting supplies, and frames. Write for information.

Gutcheon Patchworks
611 Broadway
New York, N.Y. 10012

Original design kits for patchwork quilts, crib quilts, bags, and pillows. Also quilt batting, quilt backing, and other sorts of craft and needlework kits. Write for information.

Jenny Lynn II
13410-B Preston Rd.
Dallas, Tex. 75240

Thirty cotton calico prints. Send 50¢ for swatches.

Needleart Guild
2729 Oakwood N.E.
Grand Rapids, Mich. 49505

List of 150 stencils for marking heirloom quilting patterns onto your quilt top. Also: frames, hoops, backing, batting, needles, and thread. Send 50¢ for catalogue and quilting-pattern sample.

Nimble Needle Treasures
P.O. Box 1082
Sapulpa, Okla. 74066

Quarterly magazine of news, lore, and patterns for quiltmakers.

Quality Quilting
Stover, Mo. 65078

They will machine-quilt your quilt. Send 25¢ for sample of work and information.

Quilt Country
300-A W. Eighth St.
Kansas City, Mo. 64105

They sell old and new quilts and tops and provide hand or machine quilting for your quilt. They also buy new quilts. Write for information.

Quilter's Newsletter
P.O. Box 394
Wheat Ridge, Colo. 80033

Monthly magazine of news and lore about quilts and quiltmakers. Lesson, patterns, merchandise offerings.

Quilts and Other Comforts
P.O. Box 394
Wheat Ridge, Colo. 80033

Fabrics, thread, batting, templates, quilt kits, and other supplies. Write for information.

Sears, Roebuck and Company

Quilt batting, comforter batting, quilting frames, and hoops. Look up the nearest outlet in your phone book.

Stearns & Foster Company
Quilting Department
Cincinnati, Ohio 45215

Mountain Mist quilt batting, piecework and appliqué patterns, quilting patterns, blueprints for building a quilting frame, kits for quilts and pillows. Write for information.

BIBLIOGRAPHY

Gutcheon, Beth. *The Perfect Patchwork Primer.* New York: David McKay Co., 1973.

Hinson, Dolores A. *Quilting Manual.* New York: Hearth-side Press, 1966.

Holstein, Jonathan. *The Pieced Quilt: An American Design Tradition.* Greenwich, Conn.: The New York Graphic Society, 1973.

Houck, Carter, and Myron Miller. *American Quilts and How to Make Them.* New York: Charles Scribners & Sons, 1975.

Ickes, Marguerite. *The Standard Book of Quiltmaking and Collecting.* New York: Dover Publications, 1959.

Laury, Jean Ray. *Quilts and Coverlets: A Contemporary Approach.* New York: Van Nostrand Reinhold, 1970.

McKim, Ruby. *One Hundred and One Patchwork Patterns.* New York: Dover Publications, 1962.

Orlofsky, Myron and Patsy. *Quilts in America.* New York: McGraw-Hill, 1974.

Safford, Carleton, and Robert Bishop. *America's Quilts and Coverlets.* New York: E. P. Dutton, 1972.

Schoenfeld, Susan. *Pattern Design for Needlepoint and Patchwork.* New York: Van Nostrand Reinhold, 1974.

Wooster, Ann-Sargent. *Quiltmaking: The Modern Approach to a Traditional Craft.* New York: Drake, 1972.

Index

Boldface type indicates illustration page references.